EATING
OUTDOORS

VOGUE

COOKERY COLLECTION

EATING
OUTDOORS

HAMLYN

First published in 1988 by
The Hamlyn Publishing Group
Michelin House, 81 Fulham Road
London SW3 6RB

© Bernard Leser Publications Pty Limited 1988
ALL RIGHTS RESERVED
Unauthorised reproduction or copying strictly prohibited

ISBN 0 600 55846 0

Printed in Hong Kong

Text and photographs supplied by Vogue Australia

Vogue Australia Editor-in-Chief **June McCallum**
Vogue Entertaining Guide Editor **Carolyn Lockhart**
Food Editor **Joan Campbell**

Publishers' acknowledgments
Artworks: Maggie Smith(borders), Tim Mulkern (10, 11, 60, 61); Editor Wendy Lee; Contributing Editor, Suzy Powling; Editorial Assistant, Carolyn Pyrah; Art Editor, Pedro Prá Lopez; Designer, Michelle Stamp/Crucial Books; UK Consultant, Jenni Fleetwood; Production controller, Audrey Johnston

Vogue Australia would like to thank the following for their invaluable contribution:

Janet Alstergren (Herb Scones 65); Mark Armstrong, Pegrum's, Sydney (Salad of Smoked Quail and Peach with Basil Vinaigrette 54-5); Dorothy Barlow (Veal with Green Peppercorns 78); Susy Barry (Spicy pork 24-5, Thai Salad 52, Beef Salad 57); Mogens Bay Esbensen (Walnut Bread 62, Pane di Romarino 64); Ann Bennett (Blender Mayonnaise Variations 41); George Bevan (Barbecued Squid 14, Fillet of Beef with Marrow Farce 28, Salted Potatoes 31, Whisky Oranges with Honeyed Cream 32-3, Crispy Vegetable Salad 48); Mandy Bruce (Tomato Barbecue Sauce 8, Stuffed Rolled Ham 24, Barbecued Calves Liver 24, Fresh Fruit in Champagne 93); Libby Buhrich (Watercress and Walnut Salad 47, Potato Salad with Tarragon Mayonnaise 51, Peach and Mango Salad with Passionfruit Dressing 82); Joan Campbell (Cooked Prawns in the Shell 14, Bacon-wrapped Scallop Kebabs 16, Barbecued Baby Octopus with Prawns 16-17, Oyster-stuffed Sausages 17, Roast Oysters with Three Sauces 17, Whole Barbecued Fish with Chinese Ginger Sauce 19, Seafood Trio with Garlic Lemon Butter 19, Singapore Chicken Satay 20, Butterflied Leg of Lamb 26, Lamb in Spicy Yoghurt Marinade 26, Bananas Baked in Foil 32, Warm Pineapple Dessert 32, Fresh Fig Slices with Raspberry Cream 33, French Ice-cream 34, Coconut Ice-cream 35, Pineapple and Passionfruit Pavlova 36, Chocolate Rum Cake 36, Basic Vinaigrette 40, Walnut Oil Vinaigrette 40, Peanut and Sesame Oil Vinaigrette 40, Tarragon Vinegar Dressing 40, Lemon and Coriander Dressing 40, Classic Mayonnaise 41, Cucumber and Yoghurt Salad 44, Cucumber Vinaigrette 44, Australia Salad 48, Salad of Tomato, Purple Onion and Avocado 48, Avocado, Bean Shoot and Olive Salad 48, Tomato and Bocconcino Salad 51, Prawn and Mango Salad 52, Crab Salad 53, Chicken with Water Chestnuts and White Grapes 54, Baby Cheese Scones 64, Cucumber and Watercress Sandwiches 67, Egg and Stuffed Olive Sandwiches 67, Prawn and Celery Sandwiches 67, Smoked Salmon Sandwiches 67, Pâté en Croûte 68, Crab Cream 70, Salmon and Prawn Mousse 70, Trout and Smoked Salmon Rillettes 71, Whole Duck Terrine 73, Spiced Orange Slices 73, Chicken Liver and Champagne Pâté 73, Pearl Beach Pâté 74, Pâté de Lapin 74, Pork Rillettes 74, Turkey Breast Roll with Italian Sausage Stuffing 78, Herbed Quail 78, Jambon Persillé 80, Roast Sirloin with Herb Béarnaise Sauce 80, Red Fruit Salad 82-3, Friands 85, Butter Biscuits 86, Pecan Nut Biscuits 86, Vanilla Biscuits 87, Apple Cream Tarts 87, Strawberry Grapefruit Punch 91, Sangria 92, Kir Royale 92, Champagne Punch 92, Vogue Fizz 93, Bloody Mary 94, Pina Colada 94; Joan Campbell for THE AUSTRALIAN MEAT AND LIVE—STOCK CORPORATION's Promotions in *Vogue Entertaining Guides* (Lemon Grass and Coconut Sauce 8, Baby Hamburgers on Tiny Toasted Rolls 28, Indonesian Satays 29, Watermelon Cubes in Watermelon Shell with Lemon Syrup 32, Italian Vegetable Terrine with Basil Vinaigrette 72, Italian Sweet Rice and Glacé Fruit Pie 84); Ross Campbell (Wild Apple Cooler 92, Strawberry Rum Daiquiri 94); Margaret Cannon (Mange Tout and Artichoke Salad 42, Green Salad with Bean Sprouts 42, Cherry Tomatoes Stuffed with Avocado 51, Cucumber Stuffed with Herb Cheese 51, Chicken and Honeydew Melon Salad 54, Fillet of Beef with Walnut Stuffing 80-1); Trish and Julian Canny (Salad Niçoise 52); Elizabeth Cattell (Mange Tout and Watercress Salad 42, Oyster Mushroom, Avocado and Nut Salad 49, Chicken Stuffed with Mango, Walnuts and Sultanas 76, Glazed Gammon 79); Helen Chapple (Viennese Biscuits 86); Christel Coombs, The Curry Maker, Sydney (Fresh Tomato Chutney 8); Jan Cowan (Blender Mayonnaise 41, Chicken with Pesto Mayonnaise 76, Coriander Crumbed Cutlets 78, Quince-glazed Pork with Caraway Seeds 79, Poppy Seed Cake 85, Rhubarb Cake 85); Nannette Crimmin (Green Melon with Ginger Sugar 82); Manuela Darling (Aïoli 41); Jonnine Evans (Herb Mayonnaise 41, Apple Pecan Nut Cake 85); Barbara Ferrall (Duck and Orange Salad 57); Jean Gardner (Vegetable, Fruit and Nut Salad 46); Allan Garth, Gravetye Manor (Smoked Duck with Sour Cherries 77) Tansy Good and Marc Bouten, Tansy's Restaurant, Victoria (Smoked Fillets of Whiting with Truffle Vinaigrette 19, Compote of Exotic Fruits 32, Ginger Ice-cream 34); Helen Gray (Peach Buttermilk Ice-cream 35, Spinach, Pine Nut and Mushroom Salad 47); James Halliday (Marinated Poussins 23); Lyn Hatton (Ginger Prawns 14-15); Barbara Heine (Glazed Ham 24); Jocelyn van Heyst (Devilled Barbecued Quail 23, Caramelised Oranges 82, Craigmoor Shortbread 86); Michael Hill Smith (Pithiviers 37, Green Salad with Rose Petals 43); Michael Kershaw (Lime Pickle in Lime Juice 8); Lamrock Café, Sydney (Fresh Fruit Cocktail 90); Mike Lawrence (Provençal Baguettes 66); Moira Lockhart (Baked Picnic Loaf 66); Andrew McCrone (Violet Petal and Tomato Salad 45); Carolyn McKittrick (Leek Quiche 69, Nut Wafer Biscuits 86); Sandra McLean (Melting Moments 86); Stefano Manfredi (Pizzette 68-9); Fedor Mediansky (Garlic Chicken from Thailand 22-3, Balkan Salad 47); Robert Mondavi Winery (Raspberry Sorbet 34); Sandra Nicholas (Lemon and Herb Loin of Lamb 26); Julie O'Connor and Mary Ellis (Courgette Flower Salad 44, Tuna Fish and Green Bean Salad 52); John Olsen (Roasted Pepper Salad 31); Victoria O'Neill (Salad of Walnuts and Roquefort Cheese 50); Pamela O'Sullivan (Bacon and Spinach Salad USA 57); Elise Pascoe and John Kelly (Hazelnut Oil Vinaigrette 40, Chinese Ginger Dressing 40, Spring Salad 42); Damien and Josephine Pignolet (Salad of Tomatoes and Purple Basil 44); The Ritz Hotel, London (Tie Breaker 94); Jean Marie Rouglé (Raspberry Vinegar Dressing 40); Pixie and Eddie Rourke (Wholemeal Bread 64); June Satterley (Herb Sandwiches 67); Sheraton Hong Kong Hotel and Towers (Frozen Marguerita 94); Sheraton-Wentworth Hotel, Sydney (White Bread Dough 62-3); Deane Stahmann (Skewered Chicken with Pecans 20, Pecan and Mushroom Salad 47, Pecan Terrine 75); Julie and Jay Tulloch ('Glen Elgin' Salad 56-7); Sue and Lang Walker (Fresh Fruit Compote 82); Prue Walsh (Crème de Menthe Sorbet 34, Macadamia Nut Ice-cream 35); Annabel Weedon (Roquefort Mayonnaise 41); John Whittaker (Red Wine Marinade 8); John and Margaret Woods (Mint Drink 90).

Our thanks to the following publishers and individuals for permission to reproduce these recipes:

Trinidad Chicken Breasts, Sosaties, Roasted Corn on the Cob in Herb and Mustard Butter, Salade Verte copyright (C) Pip Bloomfield and Annie Mehra from *The Gourmet Barbecue*, Thomas Nelson Australia; Pepper Salad with Capers, copyright (C) Giuliano Bugialli, *The Taste of Italy*, Stewart, Tabori & Chang/Conran Octopus, 1984; Potato Salad, copyright (C) Nancy Keesing, *Just Look Out the Window*, published by Penguin Books, permission granted by Curtis Brown (Australia) Pty Ltd, Sydney; Parmesan Herb Bread, *Gourmet Magazine*, copyright (C) 1985 by The Condé Nast Publications Inc.; Balm Ambrosia, Loving Cup, copyright (C) *Herbs and Spices* by John and Rosemary Hemphill, Lansdowne Press, 1983; White Wine with Essence of Orange from *Simca's Cuisine* by Simone Beck and Patricia Simon. Copyright (C) 1972 by Simone Beck and Patricia Simon. Reprinted by permission of Alfred A. Knopf, Inc.

Grateful thanks to the following photographers:

Peter Caine 22; Michael Cook 2, 18, 38, 55, 66, 75, 83; Clive Frost 77; John Hay 15, 54, 81, 93; Peter Johnson 35; George Seper 25, 37, 43, 45, 46, 50, 58, 63, 65, 69, 71, 88; Rodney Weidland 6, 8, 16, 17, 21, 27, 28, 30, 33, 49, 53, 56, 70, 72, 79, 84, 87, 91.

CONTENTS

INTRODUCTION

Innovation and the freshest ingredients mean barbecues and picnics with a special style

Welcome to Vogue's Cookery Collection of recipes and ideas for eating out of doors. In many countries, feasting in the open air is a time-honoured tradition. We may not be able to guarantee good weather, but the vagaries of the climate have made us endlessly versatile, able to produce a picnic or a barbecue at a moment's notice. We are fortunate in having a continual and varied supply of fresh fruit and vegetables which combine happily with fine lean meat and an abundance of fish. Such foods could have been tailor-made for alfresco eating, and here we show you how to use them as the basis for adventurous entertaining.

Today, thanks to innovative chefs, knowledgeable food writers and Cosmopolitan cooks, eating out of doors has taken on a special style. Italian-inspired entrées may be followed by a main course of Asian origin, with fresh fruit from any one of a dozen countries to finish.

This book gives you a complete guide to the pleasure of eating alfresco. Containing almost 200 easy-to-follow recipes, it also includes practical tips for packing a picnic, sensible precautions to take before barbecuing, advice on what drinks to serve, with suggestions for delicious cocktails made with or without alcohol, and ideas for mouthwatering salads. Its aim is to help you – wherever you live – enjoy the indisputable joys and rewards of entertaining out of doors. Recipes to suit every occasion whether formal or informal, small or large are included to make your eating outdoors successful and trouble free.

Everything that's best about entertaining out-of-doors comes to life when the scene is set Vogue-style – a profusion of fresh seafood, salads and sauces to stimulate and satisfy the keenest appetites.

BARBECUES

Barbecues mean outdoor entertaining
that is simple, carefree and, above all, fun

Without doubt, a barbecue is one of the friendliest ways to entertain. There is an easy informality about gathering together to watch food being cooked and all the recipes here demonstrate that many different and exciting meals are possible.

The secret of successful barbecues is good organisation. Of course, this doesn't only mean a balanced selection of appetisers, main courses, vegetables and desserts. It also calls for efficient planning of the areas where you intend to cook, eat and serve drinks with as much care as for a formal dinner party.

Today, a barbecue may vary from a built-in structure that is almost a kitchen, complete with serving tables and storage cupboards, to the simplest of portable barbecues, basically an uncovered grill set over a firebox. In between you'll find barbecues on wheeled bases and the basic hibachi where the fuel is placed in a grate rather than a firebox. A new arrival on the barbecue scene is the Japanese kamado – a large jar of double-lined terracotta with a hinged lid, the heat controlled by a vent at the bottom and a damper in the lid. Available in two sizes, it sits in a cradle on wheels, so that it can be moved around. It may also be installed as a permanent fixture. The wonderful kettle grills for covered cooking have vents to control the heat (provided either by charcoal or gas); the cover regulates heat in all weathers, while allowing you to roast, steam and smoke.

Whatever you select, the choice of fuel will make a difference to the flavour of the food. Barbecues need a bed of glowing coals which give a constant heat without flames to burn the food. Wood is

Barbecued Squid (see page 14) sums up the best of cooking over charcoal. Superbly fresh ingredients are brought to succulent perfection within minutes, served with simple accompaniments and eaten with appreciation.

one option (make sure it has not been sprayed with insecticide and is not resinous). Charcoal burns slowly and evenly. Choose from chips, which light easily but soon burn away, or, for a longer-lasting fire, use briquettes of compressed charcoal. Light the fire well in advance: wood should be glowing embers before you start, and charcoal should be an ash-grey colour in about 20 or 40 minutes respectively. A gas-fired barbecue is clean and convenient, the flames heating a bed of volcanic rock.

The Japanese kamado, a double-lined terracotta jar with a hinged lid.

Different foods require different treatments.

SEAFOOD: fish takes very little time to cook. If you are cooking several types of food, leave the fish until last, so you can give it your complete attention.

If you are using fish for skewer cooking, make sure it is large with firm flesh. Skin and fillet it then cut into cubes. When marinating large fish, make some crosswise cuts at regular intervals on both sides to allow the marinade to penetrate. Prawns may be marinated without peeling. If you do peel them, remove the digestive tract.

Marinated fish is more likely to fall apart. Place it in a hinged wire grill or wrap it in foil (which has been well oiled and has its shiny side inside) to hold it together.

If the fish has been freshly caught, don't forget to scale, gut and wash it thoroughly. Rub a little salt into the cavity and rinse well.

POULTRY AND GAME: when barbecuing chickens, birds weighing between 1 kg/2 lb and 1.5 kg/3 lb are best. Cut them in half and cook bone side down to start, then turn over. Baste often.

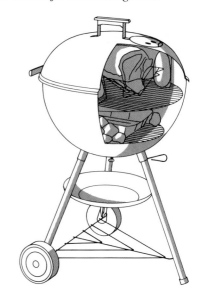

A mobile, charcoal-burning kettle barbecue with a vented lid for perfect roasting and smoke-cooking.

Ducks usually need long, slow cooking, preferably on a barbecue with a rotisserie attached (alternatively, you could try a covered or kettle-style barbecue).

Cover the breast of birds with strips of bacon or pork fat if you think they need larding. Use wire or dampened string to secure.

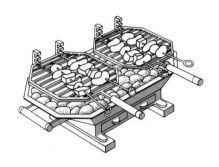

Hibachi barbecues are popular because they are simple to use and inexpensive.

A gas-fired barbecue is practical and clean. The gas quickly heats a bed of volcanic rock, meaning minimum preparation time.

Poultry is cooked when juices run clear from a small incision made near the thigh bone. Poultry must be completely cooked and the flesh should not be pink.

Marinate game before cooking to tenderise the meat and to minimise its gamey flavour.

MEAT: bring meat to room temperature before barbecuing. Rub the barbecue grill with the appropriate fat – beef fat for steaks, pork fat for spare ribs and so on – to enhance the flavour.

Make sure the juices are retained by using tongs to turn meat on barbecue, instead of anything sharp which would pierce it. Seal beef or lamb on both sides and cook rapidly if it is to be rare. For medium rare to well-done steaks, seal on both sides, then raise the grill away from the heat and cook the meat more slowly. Pork should be trimmed of excess fat and cooked over a gentle, even heat, basting frequently to retain moisture. Spare ribs should be basted and turned frequently to prevent burning. Lamb and beef spare ribs have more meat than pork spare ribs, so fewer are needed. Pork spare ribs are not so meaty – allow 450 g/1 lb per person.

Good beef cuts for barbecues are T-bone, sirloin, rump, fillet and eye rib steaks. For barbecue roasts, choose corner topside or beef strip loin. Economical cuts, to be marinated, are buttock steak, topside and silverside steak; bone-in blade, oyster blade or boneless blade steak; beef spare ribs.

Good lamb cuts for barbecues are chump, loin, and double loin chops; leg bone steaks, rib chops or cutlets. For kebabs, choose cubed boneless leg, cubed boned shoulder or meat from best end of neck. For roasts, try legs, shoulders (as they are, or boned and butterflied), racks of lamb or whole forequarters. Economical cuts are best end of neck and shoulder chops, breast of lamb.

MARINADES

Many of the cheaper cuts will taste better if you marinate them before cooking.

Marinating time varies according to the type of food and the intensity of flavour required. Meat and vegetables may be marinated for 2 hours at normal room temperature; up to 24 hours in the refrigerator. Meat which is to be tenderised in an acidic marinade can be kept in the refrigerator for up to 48 hours. Fish and shellfish should be marinated for 1 hour at room temperature; up to 2 hours in the refrigerator. There are various marinades.

- A dry marinade of crushed herbs and spices which may be blended with salt. The salt forms a brine which, when it is absorbed by the meat, carries the herb or spice flavour with it.
- A paste marinade made from fresh or dried herbs and spices, blended with a little oil and aromatic ingredients. This flavours meat in advance and keeps it moist during cooking.
- Oil-based marinades are not as dry as paste, and may be used for meat, fish and vegetables. Oil blended with aromatic ingredients will add flavour as well as protecting and enriching the meat.
- Acidic marinades are used to tenderise and may be based on wine, citrus juices, wine vinegar or yoghurt with the addition of herbs and spices and a little oil.

RED WINE MARINADE

Suitable for beef, lamb and poultry.

FOR 2-2.5 KG/4-5 LB MEAT

1 medium onion, peeled and chopped
1 medium carrot, peeled and chopped
8 juniper berries, crushed
4-6 peppercorns
mixed herbs, to taste
600 ml/1 pint red wine
1 tablespoon olive oil
250 ml/8 fl oz vinegar

Mix all the ingredients together. Herbs are optional and can be varied to suit your taste. Parsley, thyme and bay leaves are good basic flavourings.

WHITE WINE MARINADE

Suitable for pork; for lamb, substitute lemon juice for the wine vinegar and omit the coriander seeds.

FOR 2-2.5 KG/4-5 LB MEAT

500 ml/18 fl oz dry white wine
250 ml/8 fl oz white wine vinegar
5 tablespoons olive oil
3 cloves garlic, peeled and chopped
1 small carrot, peeled and sliced thinly
1 small onion, peeled and sliced thinly
4-6 peppercorns
2 bay leaves
1 teaspoon dried thyme
5 coriander seeds, crushed (optional)

Mix all the ingredients together in a bowl. Rub the meat with salt before placing it in the marinade. The meat can be left in the marinade for 2 days and should be well drained before cooking.

HERB AND LEMON MARINADE

Suitable for fish or chicken.

MAKES ABOUT 250 ML/8 FL OZ

5 tablespoons olive oil
150 ml/¼ pint white wine
juice of 1 lemon
1 onion, peeled and sliced
1 carrot, sliced
1 stalk celery, sliced
1 sprig parsley
1 bay leaf
1 tablespoon chopped fresh or 1 teaspoon dried thyme, dill or rosemary
6 peppercorns

Mix all the ingredients together. Fish should be marinated for 20-30 minutes before barbecuing. Chicken will need 1 hour or more.

LEMON GRASS AND COCONUT SAUCE

MAKES ABOUT 500 ML/18 FL OZ

1 tablespoon finely sliced lemon grass
2 cloves garlic, peeled and crushed
1 tablespoon grated ginger
2 small red chillies, sliced finely
roots from 1 bunch coriander, chopped
2 tablespoons vegetable oil
425 g/15 oz can coconut cream
3 dried Kaffir or Magrut lime leaves (from Asian food stores)
1 tablespoon nam pla (fish sauce)
1 tablespoon finely sliced coriander stems

Place the lemon grass, garlic, ginger, chillies and coriander roots in a blender and blend to a paste. Heat the oil in a saucepan over a moderate heat and fry the paste for

4-5 minutes without allowing it to brown. Break up the coconut cream and stir it into the mixture with the lime leaves. Bring the sauce to the boil, reduce the heat and cook it gently for a further 3-4 minutes. Just before serving, add the fish sauce and coriander stems, and bring the sauce back to simmering point.

TOMATO BARBECUE SAUCE

You can make this sauce the day before you wish to use it.

MAKES ABOUT 1.2 LITRES/2 PINTS

3 kg/6 lb tomatoes, chopped
1 large onion, peeled and chopped
3 medium cooking apples, peeled, cored and chopped
2 teaspoons curry powder
1 tablespoon mixed spice
6 cloves
6 peppercorns
½ teaspoon mace
½ teaspoon paprika
½ teaspoon sugar
500 ml/18 fl oz vinegar

Place all the ingredients except the vinegar in a large heavy-bottomed saucepan over a medium heat. Bring to the boil, stirring occasionally. Half cover the pan and cook slowly for 3-5 hours until the flavour is concentrated and the consistency thick. Press through a sieve or mouli into a clean pan. Add the vinegar and bring the sauce back to the boil, stirring from time to time. Leave to cook, uncovered, until the sauce has reduced to a thick consistency again. Pour into sterilised jars or bottles and cover.

FRESH TOMATO CHUTNEY

Jaggery is a crude, raw sugar available in Asian stores. The chutney keeps for 1 week.

MAKES ABOUT 1 LITRE/1¾ PINTS

4 teaspoons vegetable oil
2 bay leaves
½ teaspoon mustard seeds
½ teaspoon fenugreek seeds
8 cloves
1 whole cinnamon stick
3 teaspoons fennel seeds
¼ teaspoon red chilli powder
750 g/1½ lb tomatoes, sliced
275 g/10 oz jaggery
salt to taste

Heat the oil in a frying pan over a moderate heat. Add the bay leaves and stir for a few seconds. Add the mustard seeds, and when they start to crackle, stir in the fenugreek seeds, cloves, cinnamon stick, fennel seeds and chilli powder. Reduce the heat and cook for a few seconds. Add the tomatoes and cook until the mixture thickens to a chutney consistency. Add the jaggery and simmer over a low heat until it has dissolved. Remove the cinnamon. Season and pour into sterilised jars while hot.

LIME PICKLE IN LIME JUICE

MAKES ABOUT 600 ML/1 PINT

12 small or 6 large hot chillies
24 limes
10 cm/4 inch piece fresh ginger, peeled and cut into julienne
2 tablespoons black mustard seeds
2 tablespoons fenugreek seeds
6 bay leaves
4 tablespoons salt

If using small chillies, slit them in half. Cut large ones in strips and remove the seeds. For a very hot chutney, add the seeds of the large chillies or if you are using small chillies, leave them whole.

Cut 12 limes in quarters, discarding the seeds. Squeeze the juice from the remaining 12 limes and reserve.

Arrange a layer of limes in the bottom of a glass jar, add some chillies and ginger and a sprinkling of mustard and fenugreek seeds, a bay leaf and a pinch of salt. Repeat, layer by layer, until the jar is full. Pour in the lime juice to cover the limes. Cover the jar with a muslin cloth and stand it in a warm place. Add a pinch of salt and shake the jar each day for 4 days. Seal the jar and store it for about 6 weeks. The pickle is ready when the skins of the limes have softened and the juice has thickened.

CHUTNEYS

Although an impressive range of ready-made chutneys is available, an array of home-made relishes at a meal adds an extra personal touch – and they are very easy to prepare. Chutneys simply need long slow cooking to achieve their characteristic pulpy texture. Ingredients are mainly fruits such as apples, gooseberries, plums and tomatoes or, more adventurously, peaches and mangoes. Spices, vinegar and herbs add flavour. Dried fruits and sugar (which also preserves the fruits) sweeten the sharpness. Bottled in attractive jars, they are appetising additions at an informal outdoor meal.

BARBECUE CHECKLIST

- Invest in a barbecue trolley. Place on it everything you'll need: utensils, such as a long-handled basting brush (not plastic), long tongs, a flat metal spatula and some skewers for kebabs. Add a meat thermometer, a reliable lighter, insulated gloves or mittens, aluminium foil and hinged wire grills to hold fish or whole vegetables.
- Prepare the barbecue, placing it in a sheltered position if it is windy or if showers threaten. Check there is sufficient fuel, whichever sort you prefer, and firelighters, if necessary. Clean and oil grills and hotplates to prevent sticking.
- Light the barbecue in good time. Allow wood or charcoal to reduce to an ash-grey colour (glowing red at night) before starting to cook. There should be no flame while food is cooked.
- Check the tablesetting: provide sufficient plates, cutlery and table napkins, and prepare salt and pepper pots, fresh bread and butter.
- Make certain there is space to serve drinks, and facilities to keep them cool. There should be two glasses for each person, allowing a switch from wine to a soft drink. Have a supply of fruit juices and mineral waters to hand.
- People are naturally drawn to the barbecue as the centre of attraction. Stave off hunger pangs with a choice of light yet satisfying appetisers.
- Appetites seem to increase out of doors, so allow more food at a barbecue than you would for a meal indoors.

COOKED PRAWNS IN THE SHELL

SERVES 6

1.75 kg/4 lb medium Mediterranean prawns, cooked
4 tablespoons olive oil
2 cloves garlic, peeled and crushed finely
1 teaspoon dried oregano or 1 tablespoon finely chopped fresh oregano
freshly ground black pepper

Heat the oil in a large frying pan kept especially for the barbecue. Add the garlic, oregano, pepper and prawns. Toss about quickly over a high heat until hot. Do not cook for too long or they will toughen.

BARBECUED SQUID

SERVES 6

1 kg/2 lb squid
juice of 2 lemons
2 cloves garlic, peeled and crushed
2 tablespoons freshly chopped parsley

TO SERVE:
lemon wedges
salt and freshly ground black pepper

Clean, wash and remove the skin from the squid under running water, taking care not to lose the tentacles. Place the prepared squid in a glass bowl. Combine the lemon juice with the garlic and parsley. Pour this over the squid and leave to marinate for at least 2 hours.

Remove the squid from the marinade and drain. Bring the barbecue grill to medium heat and grill the squid and tentacles quickly, turning them 4-5 times. The outside will be crisp with soft, moist flesh inside. Serve with a squeeze of lemon juice and salt and freshly ground black pepper.

GINGER PRAWNS

SERVES 8 AS A FIRST COURSE

1 kg/2 lb uncooked prawns
120 ml/4 fl oz vegetable oil
3 tablespoons lemon juice
1 medium onion, peeled and chopped roughly
6 cloves garlic, peeled and chopped roughly
2.5 cm/1 inch piece fresh ginger, chopped roughly
2 hot green chillies or 1 teaspoon chilli powder
salt and freshly ground black pepper

GARNISH:
lemon wedges
Vietnamese mint or basil

Peel the prawns, leaving the tail tips. Slit the backs and remove the digestive tracts. Thread the prawns on to wooden skewers.

To 2 tablespoons of the oil, add the lemon juice, onion, garlic, ginger, chillies, salt and pepper, and purée to a smooth paste in a blender. Marinate the prawns in this mixture for at least 1 hour.

Cook the prawns on a pre-heated barbecue or grill, brushing with the remaining oil until cooked – about 5-8 minutes, according to size. Serve with lemon wedges and the Vietnamese mint or basil.

A sprig of Vietnamese mint highlights the exotic appeal of Ginger Prawns, presented with Oriental style.

BARBECUED BABY OCTOPUS WITH PRAWNS

If overcooked, octopus can be rather rubbery. Marinating will both tenderise it and give it flavour. If baby octopus are not available, double the quantity of prawns.

SERVES 6

24 uncooked prawns, in shells
24 baby octopus
salt and freshly ground black pepper
4 cloves garlic, peeled and crushed
500 ml/18 fl oz olive oil

TO SERVE:
lemon quarters
Tomato Barbecue Sauce (see page 13)

Wash and drain the prawns. Place in a bowl, season with salt and pepper and sprinkle with half the crushed garlic. Pour over half the olive oil.

To clean the octopus, cut the body up the centre back and remove the ink sac, digestive organs and beak. Wash well under running water and drain. Marinate in the same way as the prawns, but separately, for at least 1 hour.

Remove the prawns and octopus from their marinades and barbecue on a grill over a high heat. Do not cook for too long or they will toughen.

Serve with lemon quarters and Tomato Barbecue Sauce.

Juicy, tender Bacon-wrapped Scallop Kebabs are cooked over medium-hot coals.

BACON-WRAPPED SCALLOP KEBABS

SERVES 6

36 scallops
12 rashers bacon, rind removed
freshly ground pepper

Wash the scallops, drain them and pat dry with paper towels. Cut each bacon rasher into 3 pieces. Wrap each piece around a scallop as well as you can and thread 6 bacon-wrapped scallops on each skewer.

Barbecue over a medium heat until all the scallops are cooked through. Season with freshly ground pepper only – you will find that the salt from the bacon makes it unnecessary to add extra salt.

OYSTER-STUFFED SAUSAGES

SERVES 6

6 large, good-quality sausages
18 oysters

Barbecue the sausages carefully so that they are evenly cooked.

When they are ready, split them lengthways and fill each one with 3 oysters. Wrap the sausages in paper napkins and eat with the fingers.

ROAST OYSTERS WITH THREE SAUCES

SERVES 6

6 dozen large fresh oysters

Scrub the oyster shells clean. As soon as all the oysters are ready, place them lid side up, over a hot barbecue for no more than 2 minutes each. When the lids are open, they are ready for eating.

Transfer to individual serving dishes and serve immediately, with a selection of the following sauces as accompanying dips for the oysters.

PEPPER SAUCE

100 g/4 oz butter
juice of 2 lemons
7 drops Tabasco sauce
pinch of salt

Melt the butter in a small heavy-bottomed saucepan. Add the lemon juice, Tabasco and salt. Mix well and cook for 1 minute to blend thoroughly. Transfer to a warmed sauce bowl to serve.

LEMON SAUCE

100 g/4 oz butter
juice of 2 lemons
salt
freshly ground pepper

Heat all the ingredients together in a small saucepan, mixing well, until the butter is melted and blended with the seasoned lemon juice.

Transfer the sauce to a warmed sauce bowl to serve.

SNAIL BUTTER

100 g/4 oz butter
1 tablespoon finely chopped parsley
4 cloves garlic, peeled and crushed
salt
freshly ground pepper

Melt the butter in a small saucepan over a moderate heat. Remove the pan from the heat and add the parsley and garlic, salt and pepper. Transfer to a warmed sauce bowl and serve immediately.

Succulent Barbecued Baby Octopus with Prawns must be cooked over a high heat.

WHOLE BARBECUED FISH WITH CHINESE GINGER SAUCE

SERVES 4

1 large whole fish (red snapper, bream or John Dory), weighing about 1.5 kg/3 lb, cleaned and scaled
225 g/8 oz softened butter
salt
freshly ground black pepper
juice of 1 lemon
1 small onion, cut in fine rings

SAUCE:
cooking juices from the fish (see above)
1 tablespoon soy sauce
2 tablespoons fine julienne of fresh ginger root
2 tablespoons fine julienne of spring onions

Wash the fish and pat it dry with paper towels. Spread a third of the butter on a double layer of heavy-duty foil, add seasoning and place the fish in the middle. Put a third of the butter, more salt and pepper, the lemon juice and onion rings in the cavity of the fish. Spread the remaining butter on top with more salt and pepper.

Wrap up the foil to make a neat, well-sealed parcel. Place it on the barbecue and cook for 15 minutes on one side. Turn and cook the other side for a further 5 minutes. By this time the fish should be cooked but as heat varies in barbecues, remove the parcel to a tray, unwrap it carefully and test the thick part immediately behind the head to see if it is ready. Be careful not to spill any

Mediterranean prawns, scallops and oysters together make a Seafood Trio. Serve with Garlic Lemon Butter and few discriminating palates can resist.

juice, as this is used to make the Chinese Ginger Sauce.

When the fish is ready, lift it carefully on to a warmed serving platter using 2 fish slices. Keep warm.

Pour all the cooking juices from the barbecued fish into a small heavy-bottomed saucepan set over a high heat. Stir in the soy sauce. As soon as it starts to bubble, pour the sauce over the fish. Sprinkle with the ginger and spring onions and serve immediately.

SEAFOOD TRIO WITH GARLIC LEMON BUTTER

SERVES 4

12 large uncooked Mediterranean prawns, in the shell
12 scallops in the shell, unopened
12 oysters in the shell, unopened

GARLIC LEMON BUTTER:
100 g/4 oz butter
1 clove garlic, peeled and crushed
juice of 1 lemon
salt
freshly ground black pepper
1 tablespoon chopped parsley

Prepare the flavoured butter first. Melt the butter in a small, heavy-bottomed saucepan over a gentle heat. Add the garlic and cook gently for 2-3 minutes. Stir in the lemon juice, season to taste, and add the parsley. Place the pan to the side of the barbecue to keep warm.

Cook the shellfish directly on the hot coals of the barbecue, basting the prawns with the garlic lemon butter and spooning it into the scallops and oysters as the shells open. Remove the seafood from the heat as soon as it is cooked and serve immediately.

SMOKED FILLETS OF WHITING WITH TRUFFLE VINAIGRETTE

SERVES 6

6 large fillets of whiting
salt
freshly ground black pepper
1×25 g/1 oz can truffles

TRUFFLE VINAIGRETTE:
4 tablespoons olive oil
1 tablespoon sherry vinegar
1 tablespoon truffle juice

Season the whiting fillets lightly and smoke over a mixture of wood chips until they are tender. Drain the truffles, retaining the juice from the can.

To make the vinaigrette dressing, place the oil, vinegar and 1 tablespoon truffle juice in a screwtop jar with salt and pepper to taste. Shake well to combine all the ingredients.

Chop the truffles. When the fish is ready, transfer the fillets to individual dishes and sprinkle chopped truffle on top. Pour a little vinaigrette over each fillet and serve.

BARBECUED FISH

There is probably no better way to cook fish than over glowing charcoal, basting it frequently with lemon juice and butter or a herb butter. Fish cooks to tender perfection relatively quickly — whether little sardines, steaks of white fish or impressive pink lobsters. Serve at once.

BARBECUED POULTRY

TRINIDAD CHICKEN BREASTS

SERVES 4

4-6 chicken breasts, boned and flattened
2 tablespoons vegetable oil

STUFFING:
15 g/½ oz butter
½ onion, peeled and chopped finely
1 tablespoon soft brown sugar
2 teaspoons orange zest
juice of 1 orange
juice of ½ lemon
salt
freshly ground black pepper
450 g/1 lb sweet potatoes, cooked and mashed

BASTING LIQUID:
25 g/1 oz butter
juice of ½ lemon
juice of ½ orange
pinch of ground nutmeg
½ teaspoon ground cinnamon

Make the stuffing first. Melt the butter in a medium saucepan over a moderate heat. Fry the onion until soft and transparent. Add the sugar, orange zest, citrus juices and seasoning. Stir this mixture into the mashed sweet potato and beat well.

Lay the flattened chicken breasts on a board and divide the stuffing evenly between them. Roll them up carefully so that the stuffing does not spill out. Fasten with a small skewer.

Heat the vegetable oil in a frying pan over a moderate heat. Place the rolled chicken breasts in the pan and cook until golden brown on all sides, turning them carefully.

Remove from the pan and leave them to rest in a warm place while combining the basting ingredients. Melt the butter in a saucepan and blend in the fruit juices and spices. Remove the skewers from the rolled chicken breasts and barbecue over hot coals for 10-12 minutes, basting frequently and turning them to prevent them burning.

SKEWERED CHICKEN WITH PECANS

SERVES 6

450 g/1 lb boned chicken thighs, cut into 2.5 cm/1 inch cubes

MARINADE:
4 spring onions, chopped finely
3 teaspoons grated ginger root
1 clove garlic, peeled and crushed
1 teaspoon ground coriander
1 teaspoon five-spice powder
1 tablespoon lemon juice
120 ml/4 fl oz soured cream or yoghurt
25 g/1 oz finely chopped pecan nuts
½ teaspoon salt

Place the chicken pieces in a deep dish in which they fit comfortably in 2 layers. Combine all the marinade ingredients and mix well into the chicken. Leave for 2-3 hours or preferably overnight, stirring several times.

Thread the chicken pieces on to satay sticks which have been soaked in water for several hours. Try to keep the pieces coated in the marinade, and retain all the liquid in the dish for basting the chicken during cooking. Barbecue for 2-3 minutes on each side. Take care not to overcook.

SINGAPORE CHICKEN SATAY

MAKES 20 SATAYS

1 kg/2 lb chicken, cut into small cubes
2 cloves garlic, peeled and chopped very finely
4 small onions, peeled and grated
1 teaspoon curry powder
1 teaspoon ground cumin
1 teaspoon ground ginger
salt
4 tablespoons sugar
2 stalks lemon grass, chopped finely
65 g/2½ oz fresh ginger, grated (optional)
vegetable oil for basting

SATAY SAUCE:
8 dried red chillies
2 cloves garlic, peeled
2 small onions, peeled
4 candlenuts
3 tablespoon peanut oil
175 g/6 oz ground peanuts
3 tablespoons tamarind water or lemon juice
120 ml/4 fl oz water
4 tablespoons sugar
salt

GARNISH:
cucumber wedges

Combine the garlic, onions and spices together in a bowl, using the back of a wooden spoon to crush them as you stir. Add the salt, sugar, lemon grass and ginger if used. Stir well and add the cubed chicken. Toss the cubes to cover them with the mixture and leave for 30 minutes for the flavours to penetrate.

Caribbean-style Trinidad Chicken Breasts (pictured right) are stuffed with sweet potatoes and basted with spiced citrus juices.

TO MAKE THE SATAY SAUCE: soak the chillies in cold water to soften them. Chop them very finely together with the garlic and onion. Heat the peanut oil in a small heavy saucepan over a moderate heat and fry this mixture for 5 minutes. Stir in the peanuts and tamarind water or lemon juice. Add the water, the sugar and season with salt to taste. Bring to the boil. Reduce the heat and leave to simmer for a few minutes to thicken. Transfer the sauce to a warmed serving bowl and keep warm.

TO COOK AND SERVE: thread the chicken on to 20 satay sticks and shake off most of the flavouring ingredients. Barbecue over charcoal, basting occasionally with oil to prevent drying out. Serve with satay sauce and cucumber wedges.

DEVILLED BARBECUED QUAIL

SERVES 8

8 dressed quail split in half

MARINADE:
120 ml/4 fl oz light soy sauce
2 tablespoons honey
3-4 spring onions, chopped
2 cloves garlic, peeled and chopped
5 cm/2 inch piece root ginger, peeled and chopped
½ teaspoon five-spice powder
120 ml/4 fl oz vegetable oil
1 tablespoon walnut oil
120 ml/4 fl oz port

To make the marinade, mix the soy sauce and honey together in a bowl and add the spring onions, garlic and ginger. Add all the other ingredients and mix well.

Place the quail in a shallow casserole and cover with the marinade. Cover and leave for at least 4 hours.

Remove the quail from the marinade and pat dry with paper towels. Strain the marinade into a bowl and use to baste the quail during cooking.

Barbecue the devilled quail, turning them frequently and basting them often. They will be very tender and well browned when barbecued in this way.

Like many Oriental dishes, Garlic Chicken from Thailand needs careful surveillance to achieve perfection.

MARINATED POUSSINS

SERVES 4

4 poussins (about 400 g/14 oz each)
teriyaki sauce
4 or 5 sprigs mixed fresh herbs per bird (e.g. thyme, marjoram, rosemary, sage, parsley)
170 g/5½ oz packet wild rice
350 g/12 oz long-grain rice
¼ teaspoon powdered saffron

Clean the poussins and dry with paper towels inside and out. Marinate the poussins in the teriyaki sauce for approximately 1 hour, turning them frequently so that the sauce covers the birds. Remove the poussins from the marinade and stuff generously with herbs.

Cook the wild rice as instructed on the packet.

Place the poussins on the barbecue and cook for 15 minutes, turning frequently. Test to see if they are cooked. If your fire is low, you may find they require a little more cooking.

Cook the long-grain rice with the saffron in a large saucepan of boiling salted water. Boil for 12 minutes. Drain if necessary and arrange in the centre of a warmed platter. Place the barbecued poussins on top of the saffron rice and serve surrounded by the wild rice.

GARLIC CHICKEN FROM THAILAND

SERVES 6

1 kg/2 lb chicken breasts or thighs
1 tablespoon black peppercorns
stems of 4 whole plants fresh coriander
2.5 cm/1 inch piece fresh ginger, peeled and chopped very finely
4 cloves garlic, peeled and chopped finely
2 teaspoons salt
4 tablespoons lemon juice

Crush the peppercorns with a pestle and mortar. Wash the coriander plants very thoroughly and chop the stems finely. Combine with the ginger, garlic, salt and lemon juice. Rub into the chicken and place on a grill over glowing coals. Cook, turning frequently until tender with a crisp skin.

TASTE AND TENDERNESS

Because cooking over radiant heat is relatively fast, poultry and game must be properly prepared if they are to be as succulent as they should. Marinating for at least an hour according to size, age and the depth of flavour required is the best way of achieving this, and allows small game birds to cook successfully whole, while larger items such as chickens should be jointed or cut into small pieces. Baste frequently while cooking, making sure they cook evenly all over and at a constant temperature. Don't forget to let them rest briefly before serving and the results will be delicious.

GLAZED HAM

SERVES 20

1 large ham
good-quality marmalade
slices of fresh pineapple

GARNISH:
fresh herbs

Remove the outer skin from the ham, preferably in one piece. Cut off the excess fat, and lay the skin back over the ham until you are ready to cook it.

Remove the skin and smother the top of the ham with plenty of good-quality marmalade. Arrange slices of fresh pineapple decoratively over the ham. Place it in a prepared kettle barbecue and cook for 1 hour. Check the heat after 30 minutes and half-close the vents if it appears to be cooking too quickly.

Place the ham on a large serving platter and garnish with fresh herbs.

STUFFED ROLLED HAM

SERVES 6

6×5 mm/¼ inch slices of ham off the
* bone*
French mustard (Dijon or moutarde de
* Meaux)*

Spread each slice of ham with a little mustard. Roll up and secure with a toothpick. Barbecue over charcoal until heated through. Do not overcook or the ham will begin to dry out and become tough.

ENJOYABLE ALTERNATIVES

Although lamb and beef are frequently chosen as the most popular meats for barbecues, try some alternatives. An impressive centrepiece is a large leg of ham cooked in a kettle barbecue. Or, when last-minute entertaining arises, try slices of ham, simply spread with a little grainy mustard before rolling them up and heating them gently over the charcoal. Offal is an acquired taste, but for those who enjoy the tender texture and delicate flavour of calves liver, a variety of marinades and sauces provide options for entrées and main courses.

SPICY PORK

Spicy Pork can also be stir-fried, as shown in the picture (right).

SERVES 4

750 g/1½ lb pork fillet, cut in cubes

MARINADE:
2 tablespoons light soy sauce
freshly ground black pepper
3 cloves garlic, peeled and crushed
2 tablespoons chilli sauce
juice of 2 lemons
a little coriander (optional)

To make the marinade, mix all the ingredients together in a bowl. Place the meat in a shallow dish and spoon over the marinade. Leave for at least 2 hours, turning the meat from time to time. Remove cubes of meat from the marinade, reserving any liquid to baste the meat during cooking.

Thread the meat on to skewers. Barbecue them over hot charcoal for 10-15 minutes, turning frequently to prevent them burning and basting if necessary. Serve with Thai Salad (see page 52) and relishes.

BARBECUED CALVES LIVER

SERVES 4

450 g/1 lb calves liver, skinned and cut
* into 2.5 cm/1 inch cubes*
120 ml/4 fl oz Tomato Barbecue Sauce
* (see page 13)*

MARINADE:
juice of ½ lemon
3 tablespoons oil
1 teaspoon marjoram
1 tablespoon freshly chopped oregano or
* basil*
4 tablespoons white wine
freshly ground black pepper

To make the marinade, mix all the ingredients together in a bowl. Place the liver in a shallow dish and mix in the marinade, making sure the cubes are well covered. Leave overnight in the refrigerator.

To cook the liver, remove it from the marinade, reserving the liquid. Thread the liver on to satay sticks and barbecue over hot coals for 10-15 minutes, basting them frequently with the marinade. Serve with Tomato Barbecue Sauce.

Tender Spicy Pork finds a perfect partner in crisp and crunchy chilled Thai Salad (see page 52), with a variety of relishes to complete the menu.

LEMON AND HERB LOIN OF LAMB

SERVES 8

2 loins of lamb, bones removed
leaves from 2 sprigs of fresh thyme
leaves from 2 sprigs of fresh rosemary
grated rind of ½ lemon
juice of 1 lemon
4 cloves garlic, peeled and crushed
5 cm/2 inch piece fresh ginger, chopped
   finely
2-3 tablespoons honey
salt
freshly ground black pepper
75 g/3 oz butter
3 tablespoons olive oil

Put into a blender or food processor, the sprigs of thyme, rosemary, grated lemon rind and juice, crushed garlic, chopped ginger, honey, salt and pepper and blend thoroughly to a purée. Reserve 1 tablespoon of this lemon and herb mixture. Add butter and continue to blend. Reserve 2 tablespoons of this herb butter.

Generously spread the herb butter inside the lamb loins. Roll them up and stitch them together, using very fine string and a darning needle.

Add the olive oil to the reserved lemon herb mixture. Score the loins with a sharp knife and rub the mixture well into the meat. Put the meat into a china dish and pour over any remaining mixture. Cover and refrigerate for at least 4 hours or overnight if possible so that the flavours penetrate the meat. Turn the loins in the oil mixture occasionally.

Heat the oven to hot, 230°/450°F, Gas Mark 8, and cook the lamb on the centre shelf for approximately 20 minutes, according to how well you like it done. Finish cooking the lamb on a hot barbecue for 15 minutes, turning the loins frequently so that they are evenly crisp and are nicely browned on the outside.

TO SERVE: carve into 2.5 cm/1 inch slices and transfer to individual warmed plates. Melt the reserved herb butter and spoon over the meat.

BUTTERFLIED LEG OF LAMB

SERVES 4-6

2.5 kg/5 lb leg of lamb, boned
lemon pepper
2 cloves garlic, peeled and crushed
2 teaspoons powdered ginger
salt
freshly ground black pepper
100 g/4 oz softened butter
vegetable oil

Spread out the leg of lamb on a board, skin side down, and arrange the loose pieces to make it roughly the same thickness all the way through. To help keep it in a butterfly shape during cooking, push some long skewers through the meat to keep it rigid. Sprinkle each side with plenty of lemon pepper, garlic, ginger, salt and pepper and spread all over with softened butter.

This is best cooked in an old-fashioned hinged barbecue. If cooking on a grill over charcoal turn it carefully and often, painting with vegetable oil as you think the meat needs it. The lamb should be cooked in 45 minutes. It is ready when crisp on the outside and pink in the middle.

TO SERVE: place the meat on a board, remove the skewers and cut into slices across the narrow part.

LAMB IN SPICY YOGHURT MARINADE

SERVES 4

2 lamb rib eye (meat from boned mid-loin
   or rack)

MARINADE:
1 medium onion, peeled and sliced
1 tablespoon ground coriander
1 teaspoon salt
1 teaspoon ground cumin
¾ teaspoon black pepper
¾ teaspoon ground cloves
¾ teaspoon ground cardamom
1 teaspoon ground ginger
1 teaspoon ground cinnamon
1 teaspoon poppy seeds
25 g/1 oz butter, melted
250 ml/8 fl oz plain yoghurt
3 tablespoons lemon juice

Place all the marinade ingredients in a blender and blend until smooth. Alternatively, place in a mixing bowl and beat well until blended. Place the meat in a shallow dish and pour over half the marinade. Cover and refrigerate overnight, or let stand at room temperature for 2 hours.

Remove the meat from the marinade, reserving the liquid for basting during cooking.

Barbecue the meat over hot coals for about 20 minutes or until done to your taste, basting occasionally with the marinade. Any marinade left over may be quickly heated through and served as a sauce with the lamb.

WORLDWIDE APPEAL

Dishes from Asia are a particularly good choice for barbecues. In Japan, only the very best cuts of beef would be used, cut up into small, even dice, cooked quickly and served on skewers with a choice of side dishes. From India comes a variety of flavourful marinades and spicy sauces for tenderising chicken joints and cuts of lamb. Kebabs feature strongly in Middle Eastern cookery. Cubed meat, often lamb, is marinated first in oil and lemon juice with onions and herbs, or in yoghurt with onion juice and seasonings so that it has a delicious flavour when cooked.

SOSATIES

SERVES 8

1.75 kg/4 lb boneless lamb cut into 2.5-4 cm (1-1½ inch) cubes
1½ tablespoons vegetable oil
200 g/7 oz onions, peeled and chopped finely
½ teaspoon ground coriander
pinch of turmeric
½ tablespoon good, hot curry powder
4 tablespoons fresh lime juice, mixed with 4 tablespoons water
½ tablespoon brown sugar
1 tablespoon apricot jam
½ teaspoon salt
freshly ground black pepper
1 clove garlic, peeled and crushed
½ tablespoon sambal oelek
12 baby onions, peeled

Meticulous preparation makes each mouthful of Sosaties meltingly tender.

Start the preparation the day before the barbecue. Heat the oil in a large casserole and gently fry the chopped onions until they are soft and transparent. Add the coriander, turmeric and curry powder. Stir for 2-3 minutes. Add the lime juice and water, brown sugar and apricot jam. Continue cooking until the mixture reaches boiling point. Reduce the heat and simmer for 15 minutes. Remove from the heat and leave the mixture to cool.

Season the lamb cubes. Add the garlic, sambal oelek and lamb to the curry mixture. Marinate overnight, turning the meat occasionally.

Remove the lamb from the casserole, reserving the marinade. Thread the meat on to 6-8 skewers, alternating with the onions. Barbecue the sosaties for 8-15 minutes, depending on how well you like the lamb cooked, turning it often and basting with the leftover marinade.

FILLET OF BEEF WITH MARROW FARCE

SERVES 6

1.5 kg/3 lb fillet of beef
4 tablespoons Dijon mustard
freshly ground black pepper

MARROW FARCE:
6 marrow bone pieces each 7.5 cm/3
* inches long*
65 g/2½ oz butter
½ medium onion, peeled and
* chopped*
4 small mushrooms, chopped

TO MAKE THE MARROW STUFFING: soak the marrow bones in water for 1 hour. Drain and place in a saucepan with enough salted water to cover. Bring to the boil. Drain and carefully remove the marrow from the bones with a small teaspoon.

Melt the butter in a small saucepan. Fry the onion until soft. Add the mushrooms and cook gently for 2 minutes. Add the prepared marrow.

TO STUFF AND COOK THE MEAT: remove all sinew and fat from the beef. Carefully cut a pocket lengthways in the beef, deep enough to hold the stuffing, making sure not to cut through each end. Place the stuffing evenly in the pocket and tie the meat at regular intervals with fine string to secure. Coat the beef with Dijon mustard and season with pepper.

Barbecue the beef over a medium heat for 12-16 minutes, turning on all sides until browned but still rare. Allow to stand in a warm place for 10 minutes. Remove the string and cut the meat diagonally into thick slices to serve.

BABY HAMBURGERS ON TINY TOASTED ROLLS

SERVES 8

HAMBURGERS:
1 kg/2 lb fine steak mince
1 large onion, peeled and chopped finely,
* fried in butter*
20 g/¾ oz chopped parsley
2 teaspoons French mustard

1 tablespoon tomato sauce
1 tablespoon Worcestershire sauce
2 eggs
salt and freshly ground pepper
a little oil

TO SERVE:
6 small onions, peeled
small bread rolls
butter
tomato sauce

Rare Fillet of Beef with Marrow Farce needs only a garnish of fresh herbs.

TO MAKE THE HAMBURGERS: mix together the minced steak, prepared onion, parsley, mustard, tomato and Worcestershire sauces, eggs, and salt and pepper, and form into baby hamburgers. Set aside. Slice the onions in rings and cut the bread rolls in half. Cook the hamburgers and onion rings on the oiled plate of a gas barbecue.

TO SERVE: when the hamburger and onions are cooked, toast the halved bread rolls and spread them with butter. Place a small hamburger on each half roll and top with a pile of onion rings. Serve with tomato sauce.

KOREAN BEEF SPARE RIBS

SERVES 6-8

2 kg/4 lb beef short ribs cut into 7.5 cm/3 inch lengths

MARINADE:
120 ml/4 fl oz soy sauce
120 ml/4 fl oz water
4 tablespoons finely chopped spring onions
2 teaspoons finely grated garlic
1 teaspoon finely grated fresh ginger
1 tablespoon brown sugar
½ teaspoon ground black pepper
2 tablespoons sesame seeds, toasted and crushed
2 tablespoons medium dry sherry

Slash the meat nearly to the bone. Combine the marinade ingredients. Add the ribs, mix well and marinate in the refrigerator, at least overnight, for 24 hours if possible.

To cook, place the meat on the barbecue grill with the bone side downwards and cook until brown. (These ribs need to be cooked slowly.) Turn and cook the other side until well done. Turn the pieces frequently until they are all brown and crisp.

INDONESIAN SATAYS

SERVES 8

1 kg/2 lb beef eye of blade steak, cut into cubes

MARINADE:
1 tablespoon palm or brown sugar
1 tablespoon oil
2 tablespoons soy sauce
½ teaspoon salt
1 teaspoon ground cumin or coriander
3 cloves garlic, peeled and crushed
2 teaspoons grated fresh ginger
2 dried chillies, crumbled

SATAY SAUCE:
2 tablespoons peanut oil
1 onion, peeled and chopped finely
4 cloves garlic, peeled and crushed
2-4 baby chillies, according to taste, chopped finely
1 teaspoon blachan (shrimp paste)
2 tablespoons light soy sauce
1 teaspoon tamarind essence
375 g/13 oz crunchy peanut butter
1 tablespoon palm or brown sugar
4 tablespoons boiling water

TO SERVE:
50 g/2 oz coconut cream
4 tablespoons single cream

TO MARINATE: thread the meat on bamboo skewers and place in a shallow dish. Combine all the marinade ingredients and pour them over the meat. Leave to marinate for at least 12 hours.

TO MAKE THE SATAY SAUCE: heat 1 tablespoon of oil in a frying pan over a moderate heat. Cook the onion until it is soft and golden. Add the garlic and let it brown slightly. Remove the onion and garlic from the pan. Add the remaining oil and fry the chillies for

5 minutes. Add the blachan to the pan and cook for a further 2 minutes before returning the onion and garlic to the pan. Stir in the soy sauce, tamarind essence, peanut butter, sugar and boiling water and cook together for 15 minutes, stirring occasionally. You can now bottle the sauce and, once cool, store it in the refrigerator until ready to use.

TO SERVE: break the coconut cream in to small chunks and heat it with the single cream in a small saucepan over a moderate heat, stirring until the coconut cream melts. Place 250 ml/8 fl oz of satay sauce in a serving bowl and stir in the cream mixture. Taste, and add more sugar and tamarind essence if necessary. The sauce is served at room temperature, not hot.

Remove the satays from the marinade and cook on a hibachi barbecue over hot coals, turning once. Serve with the sauce.

INDONESIAN IDEAS

Indonesian food is extremely varied and full of flavour. To accompany a satay dish serve plain boiled rice and pieces of refreshing cucumber. The main dish may be chicken heavily flavoured with garlic, beef with chillies or crab with ginger. More rice, cooked with a little saffron, complements a salad of raw pickled vegetables, such as carrots, cauliflower florets, courgettes and baby sweetcorn, in colour, texture and flavour. Mix shredded lettuce, curly endive, sliced onion, sweet pepper, shrimp and croûtons for an accompanying side salad.

ROASTED CORN ON THE COB IN HERB AND MUSTARD BUTTER

Start preparation 2 hours before serving.

SERVES 8

8 ears of corn

HERB AND MUSTARD BUTTER:
1 teaspoon French mustard
225 g/8 oz unsalted butter, softened
2 tablespoons finely chopped parsley
2 tablespoons finely chopped chives
2 tablespoons finely chopped shallots
2 teaspoons fresh lemon juice
½ teaspoon salt
freshly ground black pepper

To make the herb and mustard butter, combine all the ingredients in a glass or ceramic bowl. Cover and chill for 1-2 hours.

Peel back the corn husks but do not remove them. Remove the silk. Soak the husks in water.

Take the herb butter out of the refrigerator and bring back to room temperature. Beat the butter until it is fluffy and soft. Spread each ear of corn with 1 tablespoon of the butter. Wrap the corn in the husks and then in foil.

Roast on a grill over hot glowing coals for about 10-15 minutes or until the corn is tender, turning it often. Unwrap the corn from the foil, remove the husks and serve with the remaining herb and mustard butter.

An appetising addition to any barbecue, corn on the cob ready for roasting with an interesting herb and mustard butter.

SALTED POTATOES

SERVES 8

8 medium potatoes
3 tablespoons sea salt
225 g/8 oz butter
250 ml/8 fl oz soured cream
2 tablespoons chopped chives

Scrub the potatoes and roll them in salt while they are still wet. Wrap each one tightly in foil. Cook them at the edge of the barbecue grill for 50 minutes-1 hour, turning them once. Alternatively place them in the glowing charcoal for 20 minutes. Unwrap the cooked potatoes and make a cross cut in the top. Serve the butter, soured cream and chives in separate bowls.

GARLIC BREAD

As an alternative to garlic, flavour the butter with a mixture of fresh chopped herbs.

MAKES 1 FRENCH STICK

1 French bread stick
100 g/4 oz softened butter, or to taste
2-3 cloves garlic, according to taste, peeled and chopped finely

Heat the oven to moderately hot, 190°C/375°F, Gas Mark 5.

Cut the bread into thin diagonal slices, almost through to the bottom crust but stopping just short so the stick holds together.

In a bowl cream the butter and blend in the garlic. Spread the cut surfaces of the bread with the garlic butter. Wrap the loaf in foil. Bake it in the oven for 15 minutes, then loosen the foil and bake the loaf for a further 4-5 minutes to crisp the crust. Keep warm on the barbecue until required.

ROASTED PEPPER SALAD

SERVES 6

3 sweet red peppers

VINAIGRETTE:
3 tablespoons olive oil
1 tablespoon lemon juice
1 tablespoon freshly chopped fines herbes (such as parsley, chives and basil)

GARNISH:
12 anchovy fillets
100 g/4 oz black olives

Roast the whole peppers over a charcoal fire, turning them regularly until they are evenly black on the outside. Remove them from the grill and cover with a towel for 5 minutes to rest. Scrape off the blackened skin. Rinse the peppers carefully under gently running water and pat dry. Cut off the tops and remove the seeds, being sure to save the juices.

Place the ingredients for the vinaigrette dressing in a screwtop jar and shake well to blend. To assemble the salad, slice the peppers in half lengthways and arrange them on a plate with the hollow side up. Pour over the juices from the peppers, together with the vinaigrette and let the salad stand for 1 hour in a cool place (not the refrigerator). Serve garnished with anchovy fillets and black olives.

DESSERTS FOR BARBECUES

BANANAS BAKED IN FOIL

SERVES 6

6 bananas, peeled
75 g/3 oz brown sugar
1½ teaspoons ground cinnamon
3 tablespoons Grand Marnier
50 g/2 oz soft butter
250 ml/8 fl oz single cream

Spread out a piece of heavy-duty foil for each banana. Place 1 banana on each piece of foil and sprinkle with sugar, cinnamon and half a tablespoon of liqueur. Place a dot of butter on top. Wrap up into neat parcels and barbecue for 15 minutes over a medium heat, turning frequently. Remove from the parcels and serve with cream.

COMPÔTE OF EXOTIC FRUITS

SERVES 8

1 papaya
1 mango
4 kiwifruit
4 fresh lychees
1 pineapple
4 passionfruit
lime juice
100 g/4 oz caster sugar
350 ml/12 fl oz Sauternes or champagne

TO SERVE:
Ginger Ice-cream (see page 34)

Prepare each fruit according to type and arrange in slices in a bowl. Pour over the lime juice. Sprinkle the sugar evenly over the fruits and pour the wine over all. Leave to macerate, covered, for at least 2 hours. Serve with Ginger Ice-cream.

WATERMELON CUBES IN WATERMELON SHELL WITH LEMON SYRUP

SERVES 8-10

1 large watermelon
250 ml/8 fl oz water
100 g/4 oz sugar
juice of 2 lemons
zest of 1 lemon

TO SERVE:
1 lemon, sliced thinly
crushed ice

Cut the watermelon in half lengthways and carefully cut out the flesh, leaving the shells intact. Discard the seeds and and cut the watermelon flesh into cubes. Return the cubes to the shells and leave in a cool place. TO MAKE THE SYRUP: place the water, sugar, lemon juice and zest in a small saucepan set over a moderate heat. Stir constantly until the sugar has completely melted. Remove the pan from the heat and leave the syrup to cool completely.
TO SERVE: pour the lemon syrup over the watermelon cubes and decorate them with lemon slices. Spoon over the crushed ice and serve immediately.

WARM PINEAPPLE DESSERT

SERVES 6-8

1 large ripe pineapple
2 tablespoons brown sugar
120 ml/4 fl oz dark rum

Remove the green top and place the pineapple on the barbecue, as far away from the flame as possible. Turn the pineapple so that it cooks on all sides. The object is to heat it through, and as this is done so slowly, the pineapple will appear to be very ripe when cooking is finished. Cook for 1 hour or more if necessary. The outside of the skin should be well scorched but not burnt.

Mix the brown sugar in a jug with the rum. Peel and slice the hot pineapple and serve on individual plates with a little of the mixture poured over each slice.

WHISKY ORANGES WITH HONEYED CREAM

SERVES 6

6 large oranges
175 g/6 oz sugar
120 ml/4 fl oz water
120 ml/4 fl oz Scotch whisky
cumquats preserved in whisky (optional)

Peel the oranges, removing all the pith, and arrange the slices in a serving dish. Place the sugar and water in a saucepan and bring to the boil, stirring. Reduce the heat and simmer for 2 minutes. Remove from the heat and stir in the whisky. Leave to cool. Pour the whisky-flavoured syrup over the orange slices and chill in the refrigerator for at least 1-2 hours. Add a few slices of cumquats preserved in whisky to the dish if desired. Serve with Honeyed Cream (see page 33).

HONEYED CREAM

250 ml/8 fl oz double cream
3 tablespoons Scotch whisky
3 teaspoons clear honey

Whip the cream lightly in a bowl. Mix the honey and whisky together, fold into the cream and beat until thick.

FRESH FIG SLICES WITH RASPBERRY CREAM

SERVES 6

9 large ripe figs, sliced across
250 ml/8 fl oz water
225 g/8 oz sugar
juice of ½ lemon
250 ml/8 fl oz whipping cream
175 g/6 oz of raspberries
caster sugar to taste

Arrange the fig slices on a dish. Place the water, sugar and lemon juice in a small saucepan. Bring to the boil, stirring, and boil for 5 minutes. Leave to cool. When the syrup is quite cold, pour it over the figs. Cover and stand in the refrigerator for 1 hour.

TO SERVE: arrange the figs on individual plates and spoon over a little syrup. Whip the cream lightly. Break up the raspberries and sprinkle them with the sugar. Add them to the cream. Spoon the mixture into the centres of the figs.

Whisky Oranges with Honeyed Cream makes a tantalising blend of sweet and sharp.

RASPBERRY SORBET

The amount of sugar used in a fresh fruit sorbet depends upon the sweetness of the fruit. Use enough to give a smooth texture, but not so much that the sorbet tastes more of sugar than the fruit.

SERVES 10

1.25 kg/2½ lb raspberries
juice of ½ lemon
approximately 275 g/10 oz caster sugar

Purée the raspberries in a food processor or put them through the fine plate of a food mill. Press the purée into a bowl through a fine sieve to remove all the seeds. Whisk in the lemon juice and sugar.

The sweetened purée should be slightly sweeter than you would want the frozen sorbet to taste.

Freeze the mixture in an ice-cream maker. Alternatively, pour it into a cake tin and freeze until mushy. Transfer the half-frozen mixture to a baking sheet, cover with foil and freeze.

Serve the raspberry sorbet when it is just set with crisp dessert biscuits.

CRÈME DE MENTHE SORBET

SERVES 6

185 g/6 oz caster sugar
500 ml/18 fl oz water
½ teaspoon gelatine, softened in 2
  teaspoons water
30 fresh mint leaves
120 ml/4 fl oz strained lemon juice
2 tablespoons crème de menthe
  liqueur
green colouring
2 egg whites

Place the sugar and water in a saucepan and bring to the boil. Mix in the gelatine. Place in a blender with the mint leaves, lemon juice, crème de menthe and a few drops of green colouring, and blend well. Pour the mixture into a cake tin and freeze until it becomes mushy.

Transfer the half-frozen sorbet to a bowl. Beat the egg whites until stiff and fold them into the sorbet mixture. Put in to a flat tray, cover with foil and freeze.

Sorbets are best served when only just set. They are inclined to get hard and lose some of their flavour if left too long in the freezer. If this should happen, you can easily soften them to the right consistency by putting a small quantity at a time into a food processor.

FRENCH ICE-CREAM

SERVES 6

150 g/5 oz caster sugar
5 egg yolks
1 vanilla pod
600 ml/1 pint single cream

Beat together the sugar and egg yolks until the mixture is pale and has reached the 'ribbon' stage. Break up the vanilla pod and put the pieces in a heavy-bottomed saucepan with the cream. Place over a gentle heat and bring the cream slowly to the boil, stirring occasionally. Pour the hot cream on to the egg and sugar mixture in a thin stream, stirring constantly. Return the mixture to the saucepan and cook gently, still stirring, until the custard coats the back of a wooden spoon. Do not allow it to boil or the custard will curdle.

Carefully strain the custard into a bowl and leave it to cool. Cover and chill in the refrigerator for 1 hour before freezing in an ice-cream maker if you have one.

Alternatively pour the cold cream into a cake tin, cover with foil, and place in the freezing compartment of the refrigerator. When the cream is well set around the edges, remove the tin from the freezer and beat the cream well. Return the tin to the freezer, and leave the cream to set. Remove from the freezer and beat the cream a second time. Cover with foil and return to the freezer to freeze and store until needed.

GINGER ICE-CREAM

SERVES 8

250 ml/8 fl oz milk
250 ml/8 fl oz single cream
3 pieces preserved ginger, drained
5 egg yolks
100 g/4 oz caster sugar
1 tablespoon grated fresh ginger

Place the milk, cream and preserved ginger in a heavy-bottomed saucepan over a moderate heat. Bring just to the boil, stirring occasionally. Remove from the heat and leave to cool.

Whisk the egg yolks and sugar together until they have reached the 'ribbon' stage.

Strain the milk and cream into a clean pan and heat through. Pour the hot mixture in a thin stream over the eggs and sugar, stirring constantly. Strain the mixture back into the pan and cook over a moderate heat, still stirring, until the custard coats the back of a wooden spoon.

Pour the custard into a bowl and leave it to cool, stirring occasionally. Add the fresh ginger. Pour the mixture into an ice-cream maker and freeze.

For instructions on freezing in a refrigerator, see the method for French Ice-cream (above).

PEACH BUTTERMILK ICE-CREAM

SERVES 10

PEACH PURÉE:
*3-4 fresh yellow peaches or enough to
  make 500 ml/18 fl oz purée
40 g/1½ oz sugar*

ICE-CREAM BASE:
*1 teaspoon gelatine
150 g/5 oz sugar
600 ml/1 pint buttermilk
3 large egg yolks
¼ teaspoon salt
500 ml/18 fl oz double cream, whipped
1 tablespoon vanilla essence*

TO MAKE THE PEACH PURÉE: place the peaches in a bowl of boiling water for 1 minute. The skins should slip off easily. Halve the peaches and remove the stones. Place the sugar and peach halves in a saucepan, with just enough water to cover them. Poach gently, but do not overcook; the peaches should still have some texture. Purée in a blender or push through a sieve. Put it aside to cool.

TO MAKE THE ICE-CREAM: mix the gelatine and sugar together in a heavy-bottomed saucepan. Stir in the buttermilk and simmer over a low heat until the gelatine has dissolved. Beat the egg yolks in a bowl and add the hot buttermilk in a thin stream, still beating. Pour into the sauce and set over a low heat. Cook, stirring with a wooden spoon, until the mixture has thickened slightly. Do not boil. Blend in the salt, cream and vanilla. Turn the mixture into a bowl and chill for 1 hour. Fold in the peach purée. Freeze in an ice-cream maker. For instructions on freezing in a refrigerator, see French Ice-cream (page 34).

Allow the ice-cream to rest in the refrigerator for 30 minutes before serving.

Macadamia Nut Ice-cream (right) *with Crème de Menthe Sorbet.*

MACADAMIA NUT ICE-CREAM

SERVES 6-8

*175 g/6 oz salted macadamia nuts
500 ml/18 fl oz single cream
450 g/1 lb caster sugar
4 eggs, separated
6 tablespoons white rum or 4 tablespoons
  brown rum
2 teaspoons vanilla essence*

Pulverise the nuts in a blender. Alternatively, put them in a plastic bag and crush them with a rolling pin.

Place the cream in a double boiler and heat gently without boiling. Add the sugar and stir well to dissolve. Beat the egg yolks in a bowl and add them to the sweetened cream, stirring well with a wooden spoon until the mixture has thickened.

Pour the mixture into a large bowl and stir in the nuts. Beat the egg whites in a bowl until they form stiff peaks. Fold the egg whites into the mixture and leave it to cool. When cool, stir in the rum and vanilla essence. Pour into a shallow bowl, cover with foil and place in the freezer until firm.

COCONUT ICE-CREAM

SERVES 6

*2 × 200 g/7 oz blocks coconut cream
200 ml/⅓ pint single cream
200 g/7 oz sugar
250 ml/8 fl oz water
6 egg yolks
vanilla essence, to taste*

TO SERVE:
*tropical fruits, such as pineapple, kiwifruit
  and papaya, prepared according to type
  and sliced*

Break the coconut cream into chunks and combine with the cream in a saucepan. Heat gently, stirring, until the coconut cream dissolves and the mixture is thick and creamy. Set aside.

Place the sugar and water in a large saucepan and bring to the boil, stirring constantly. Place the egg yolks in a mixing bowl and whisk well while gradually pouring in the hot syrup. Continue beating until the mixture is white and fluffy. Blend in the coconut cream mixture and cook over a low heat until the mixture coats the back of a wooden spoon. Leave to cool and add vanilla essence to taste. Pour into an ice-cream maker and freeze.

For instructions on freezing in a refrigerator, see French Ice-cream (see page 34).

Serve with the fruit of your choice.

PINEAPPLE AND PASSIONFRUIT PAVLOVA

SERVES 10

PAVLOVA:
6 egg whites
¼ teaspoon salt
450 g/1 lb caster sugar
1 tablespoon cornflour
2 teaspoons vinegar
1 teaspoon vanilla essence

PINEAPPLE TOPPING:
6 egg yolks
50 g/2 oz sugar
2 tablespoons cornflour
juice and rind of 1 lemon
1×410 g/14½ oz can crushed pineapple
* including juice*
2 tablespoons butter
300 ml/½ pint double cream

TO DECORATE:
6-8 passionfruit
caster sugar

TO MAKE THE PAVLOVA: beat the egg whites with the salt until they hold stiff peaks. Gradually add 225 g/8 oz sugar and beat until the mixture resembles a shiny meringue. Fold in the remaining sugar, cornflour, vinegar and vanilla. Wet a piece of greaseproof paper and spread it on a baking sheet, wet side up. Pile the mixture in the middle and spread it into a circle. Cook on the centre shelf of a pre-heated very cool oven, 125°C/250°F, Gas Mark ½, for 1½ hours. Remove the baking sheet from the oven and allow to stand until cold. (If the pavlova is not to be used straight away, it must be stored in an airtight container as it will soften very quickly.)

TO MAKE THE PINEAPPLE TOPPING: mix the egg yolks, sugar, cornflour and lemon juice and rind, and beat well together. Add the pineapple and juice. Cook over a low heat until the mixture is thick and it boils. Remove from the heat and beat in the butter. Transfer to a bowl and allow to become quite cold. Whip the cream and fold it into the pineapple mixture. Spread it carefully over the pavlova just before serving.

TO DECORATE: remove the pulp and seed from the passionfruit and add a little sugar to taste. Pour over the pavlova.

CHOCOLATE RUM CAKE

SERVES 8

175 g/6 oz raisins
225 g/8 oz butter
225 g/8 oz sugar
½ teaspoon cinnamon
½ teaspoon ground cloves
3 large tablespoons cocoa
¼ teaspoon salt
300 ml/½ pint water
1 teaspoon bicarbonate of soda
4 tablespoons rum
75 g/3 oz finely chopped pecan nuts
225 g/8 oz plain flour

ICING:
150 ml/¼ pint single cream
150 g/5 oz dark chocolate, broken into
* small pieces*
25 g/1 oz butter
2 tablespoons rum

TO MAKE THE CAKE: place the raisins, butter, sugar, spices, cocoa and salt in a medium saucepan with 300 ml/½ pint cold water. Stir over a moderate heat to combine all the ingredients and bring to boiling point. Cook for 5 minutes. Remove the pan from the heat. Dissolve the bicarbonate of soda in a little warm water and add it to the mixture.

Stir in the rum and pecan nuts. Sift in the flour and beat all together with a wooden spoon. Transfer the mixture to a well-oiled ring tin and bake on the centre shelf of a pre-heated, moderately hot oven 190°C/375°F, Gas Mark 5 for 45 minutes. Immediately turn the cake out on to a wire rack to cool for at least 2-3 hours.

TO MAKE THE ICING: heat the cream, without boiling, in a small saucepan over a moderate heat. Remove from the heat and add the chocolate. Stir to melt chocolate. When it has melted completely, add the butter and stir in the rum carefully so that bubbles do not form. Let the icing stand until it is cool and firms to a spreadable consistency.

TO ICE THE CAKE: pour the icing over the cake and spread evenly with a spatula. Transfer to a flat plate and place in the refrigerator for 30 minutes to firm the icing.

ALFRESCO DESSERTS

Eating out of doors sharpens even the dullest appetite. Many guests who would often refuse the dessert course at a conventional dinner table are delighted to be offered a bowl of home-made ice-cream, fruits in syrup or a slice of irresistible cake. Desserts that can be prepared well in advance and are not tricky to serve or eat are best. This is where cakes come into their own. Macaroons, coffee walnut cake, coconut sponge darioles and apfelstrudel are firm favourites and it is hard to pass up a first-class old-fashioned fruit cake. Alternatively, fresh fruits in a pastry shell with a syrup glaze look magnificent.

PITHIVIERS

SERVES 8

2×375 g/12 oz packets puff pastry
1-2 eggs, beaten, to glaze
icing sugar for dusting

FILLING:
1 portion crème pâtissière (see below)
*200 g/7 oz freshly ground, unblanched
  almonds*
200 g/7 oz pure icing sugar, sifted
2 eggs, beaten
½ teaspoon almond essence, or to taste
1 tablespoon Cointreau, or to taste

CRÈME PÂTISSIÈRE:
3 egg yolks
50 g/2 oz caster sugar
½ teaspoon vanilla essence
45 g/1¾ oz plain flour
250 ml/8 fl oz milk

TO MAKE THE CRÈME PÂTISSIÈRE: whisk together the egg yolks, sugar and vanilla. Gradually beat in the flour until the mixture is quite smooth. Heat the milk gently in a saucepan and, when it is nearly boiling, gradually whisk it into the yolk mixture. Pour into a clean saucepan and stir over a low heat until the mixture thickens (about 2 minutes). Leave to cool.

TO MAKE THE FILLING: when the crème pâtissière is cold, mix in the almonds, icing sugar, eggs, almond essence and Cointreau. Set aside.

TO MAKE THE CAKE: heat the oven to hot, 220°C/425°F, Gas Mark 7. On a lightly floured board, roll out each packet of pastry to a size that will cut into a circle with a 28 cm/11 inch fluted flan tin.

Place 1 circle of pastry on a baking sheet, brush with beaten egg and prick with a fork. Mound the filling on the pastry, leaving a 2.5

One of the prettiest French confections, Pithiviers is best served still warm.

cm/1 inch border. Place the second circle of pastry on top, prick with a fork and brush with beaten egg (do not get any egg on the cut edge of pastry).

With a sharp knife, lightly trace a decorative pattern on top, drawing semi-circles in a spiral shape from the centre to the edge of the cake. Arrange pastry roses and leaves in the centre and paint with beaten egg.

Bake in the oven for 10 minutes. Reduce to moderately hot, 200°C/400°F, Gas Mark 6, and cook for 20-30 minutes or until the pastry is crisp and golden brown. Dust with icing sugar and serve.

SALADS

Crisp and colourful ingredients are combined in fresh, enticing summer salads

S alads for outdoor entertaining give a refreshing contrast in texture and colour. Serve them as fresh and crisp as possible. Cooked vegetable salads should be dressed while warm, and left to absorb the flavour. Leafy vegetables, celery and spring onions should be washed, dried and refrigerated in polythene bags to retain crispness until serving time. Take salads to the picnic or barbecue area in rigid polythene containers or bags. Dressings should be transported separately in firm screwtop jars.

Stock your store cupboard with a variety of oils and vinegars to ring the changes with different dressings for different salads. Always have a top-quality olive oil, dark green in colour, strong in flavour. Walnut, hazelnut and sesame seed oils have deliciously nutty flavours and will keep up to 6 months in the refrigerator, once opened. Blander oils such as safflower, sunflower, peanut and corn make good vinaigrettes when mixed with various mustards and perhaps a dash of garlic.

Have on hand a choice of vinegars, too. Malt, wine and cider vinegars are staples and balsamic vinegar is a good addition. Herb and fruit varieties may be home-made and can also be found at good delicatessens.

Remember that many salads will be enhanced with a croûton garnish. Fry tiny bread cubes in oil until golden brown, drain them on paper towels, then store in an airtight container until needed. For garlic-flavoured croûtons add 2 garlic cloves to the oil, cover and let it stand overnight before using it to fry the bread.

The composition of a colourful salad can be a work of art. Here, a glorious green selection where apparently random vegetables and flowers nestle on a bed of leaves and stems, Spring Salad (see page 42) has been arranged with minute care.

SALAD DRESSINGS

BASIC VINAIGRETTE

MAKES 250 ML/8 FL OZ

1/2 teaspoon salt
freshly ground black pepper
1 teaspoon French mustard
1 clove garlic, crushed with skin left on
4 tablespoons wine vinegar
175 ml/6 fl oz olive oil

Place salt, pepper, mustard and garlic clove in a screwtop jar. Add the vinegar and oil. Replace the lid firmly and shake the jar well to amalgamate the ingredients. If left to stand always shake well before using.

WALNUT OIL VINAIGRETTE

MAKES APPROXIMATELY 175 ML/6 FL OZ

175 ml/6 fl oz walnut oil
1 tablespoon lemon juice
1 teaspoon Dijon mustard
1 tablespoon freshly chopped chives
salt
freshly ground black pepper

Place all the ingredients in a screwtop jar. Shake well to amalgamate before serving.

HAZELNUT OIL VINAIGRETTE

MAKES 250 ML/8 FL OZ

175 ml/6 fl oz hazelnut oil
4 tablespoons white wine vinegar
salt
freshly ground black pepper

Place all the ingredients in a screwtop jar and shake until well blended. Alternatively whisk well together in a bowl.

PEANUT AND SESAME OIL VINAIGRETTE

MAKES 250 ML/8 FL OZ

175 ml/6 fl oz peanut oil
1 tablespoon sesame oil
2 tablespoons white wine vinegar
salt
freshly ground black pepper

Place all the ingredients in a screwtop jar and shake until well blended.

RASPBERRY VINEGAR DRESSING

MAKES 250 ML/8 FL OZ

5 tablespoons raspberry vinegar
5 tablespoons walnut oil
5 tablespoons peanut oil
1/2 tablespoon finely chopped shallots
1/2 tablespoon freshly chopped tarragon
1/2 tablespoon freshly chopped chives
1/2 tablespoon freshly chopped chervil
salt
freshly ground black pepper

Place all the ingredients in a large screwtop jar and shake well to amalgamate.

TARRAGON VINEGAR DRESSING

MAKES 250 ML/8 FL OZ

175 ml/6 fl oz olive oil
2 tablespoons tarragon vinegar
1-2 tablespoons lemon juice
1-2 teaspoons French mustard
salt
freshly ground black pepper

Place all the ingredients in a screwtop jar and shake until well amalgamated. Check that the strength of flavour is to your taste and adjust as necessary.

LEMON AND CORIANDER DRESSING

MAKES APPROXIMATELY 175 ML/6 FL OZ

grated roots from 1 bunch coriander
175 ml/6 fl oz peanut oil
salt
freshly ground white pepper
2 tablespoons lemon juice

Grate the coriander roots and place them in a screwtop jar with the oil and seasoning. Strain the lemon juice into a jar, put on the lid and shake well to blend before using.

CHINESE GINGER DRESSING

MAKES 250 ML/8 FL OZ

4 tablespoons preserved ginger, sliced into julienne strips
150 ml/1/4 pint peanut oil
2-3 tablespoons red wine vinegar
4 tablespoons soy sauce

Place all the ingredients in a screwtop jar and shake until well blended.

CLASSIC MAYONNAISE

MAKES 600 ML/1 PINT

6 egg yolks
1 teaspoon Dijon mustard
salt
freshly ground black pepper
1 tablespoon lemon juice
few drops garlic juice (optional)
250 ml/8 fl oz olive oil
250 ml/8 fl oz peanut oil
1 tablespoon boiling water

Place the egg yolks, mustard, salt and pepper, lemon juice and garlic juice, if used, in a bowl and beat them together with a hand-held or electric mixer until they are thoroughly mixed. Combine the two oils in a jug. Add them to the egg mixture drop by drop at first, beating all the time, then in a thin but steady stream as the mayonnaise thickens. Finally add the boiling water and transfer the mayonnaise to a jar. Cover and refrigerate.

BLENDER MAYONNAISE

MAKES 350 ML/12 FL OZ

3 egg yolks
1 tablespoon Dijon mustard
1 tablespoon white wine vinegar
salt
pepper
300 ml/½ pint peanut or olive oil

Place the egg yolks, mustard, vinegar, salt and pepper in a blender or food processor and process for a few seconds. Pour in the oil very slowly while blending at high speed, to make a thick mayonnaise.

VARIATIONS FOR BLENDER MAYONNAISE

CORAL MAYONNAISE: take the corals from 12 scallops and purée in a blender. Add to 1 quantity of freshly prepared Blender Mayonnaise.

WATERCRESS MAYONNAISE: take 1 bunch of fresh watercress, washed and blanched. Dry thoroughly on paper towels. Remove the leaves, discarding the stalks, and chop them roughly. Stir the watercress leaves into 1 quantity of fresh Blender Mayonnaise.

AÏOLI

(Garlic Mayonnaise)

MAKES 600 ML/1 PINT

2 egg yolks
1 tablespoon French mustard
juice of 1 or 2 lemons
salt
freshly ground black pepper
2 cloves garlic, peeled and crushed
500 ml/18 fl oz olive oil

Place the egg yolks, mustard, 1 tablespoon of lemon juice, salt, pepper and garlic in a food processor and process. With the motor still running, gradually add the olive oil in a steady stream until the consistency is thick and creamy. If the mayonnaise seems to be getting too thick, add a few drops of lemon juice from time to time while blending in the olive oil. Taste for salt, pepper and lemon juice.

HERB MAYONNAISE

MAKES 350 ML/12 FL OZ

3 egg yolks
1 teaspoon salt
freshly ground black pepper
1 tablespoon Dijon mustard
1-2 tablespoons lemon juice
300 ml/½ pint sunflower oil
4 tablespoons chopped mixed herbs

Place the egg yolks, salt, pepper, mustard and half the lemon juice in a blender or food processor and process briefly. With the motor running, add the oil very slowly in a thin steady stream. If the mayonnaise becomes too thick, add a few drops of lemon juice with the oil. Stir in the herbs. Check the seasoning and add more lemon juice if necessary.

ROQUEFORT MAYONNAISE

MAKES 300 ML/½ PINT

100 g/4 oz Roquefort cheese, diced
250 ml/8 fl oz Classic Mayonnaise (left)
2 teaspoons freshly chopped parsley
¼ teaspoon Worcestershire sauce
120 ml/4 fl oz single cream
2 teaspoons lemon juice
1 teaspoon grated onion
¼ teaspoon garlic salt
salt and freshly ground black pepper
cayenne

Mash the cheese with a fork. Add the mayonnaise and beat until smooth. Stir in the parsley, Worcestershire sauce and cream. When they are well blended, stir in the lemon juice, onion and garlic salt. Season with salt and pepper and transfer to a bowl. Dust lightly with cayenne and serve.

LIGHT SALADS

MANGE TOUT AND WATERCRESS SALAD

SERVES 6

100 g/4 oz mange tout
1 punnet mustard cress
leaves from 1 bunch watercress, washed
* and drained*
450 g/1 lb cherry tomatoes
120 ml/4 fl oz Basic Vinaigrette (page 40)

Bring a large pan of salted water to the boil and blanch the mange tout for 2-3 minutes. Drain, refresh under cold running water and set aside to drain thoroughly.

Cut the mustard and cress into a salad bowl. Add the watercress leaves, cherry tomatoes and mange tout. Pour over the vinaigrette dressing, toss the salad and serve immediately.

MANGE TOUT AND ARTICHOKE SALAD

SERVES 6

100 g/4 oz mange tout
6 fresh or canned artichoke hearts, sliced
juice of ½ lemon (see method)
1 teaspoon freshly chopped tarragon
120 ml/4 fl oz Basic Vinaigrette (see page
* 40)*

Steam the mange tout until just tender but still fresh in colour. Leave to cool.

Place the artichoke hearts in a salad bowl. If you are using fresh ones, pour over the lemon juice to prevent discoloration. Sprinkle with tarragon. Add the mange tout.

Pour over the vinaigrette dressing. Toss the ingredients lightly together and serve the salad immediately.

SPRING SALAD

SERVES 8

1 small red mignonette lettuce, well
* washed and crisped in the refrigerator*
1 small chicory
50 g/2 oz rocket leaves, freshly picked
small bunch watercress
8 baby nasturtium leaves
25 g/1 oz chervil sprigs
25 g/1 oz lamb's lettuce

GARNISH:
1 sweet red pepper
½ sweet yellow pepper (optional)
8 freshly picked violets
8 baby yellow tomatoes

HAZELNUT VINAIGRETTE:
4 tablespoons hazelnut oil
1 teaspoon white wine vinegar
salt
freshly ground black pepper

Wash all the salad greens in cold water and pat them dry on a clean tea towel or paper towels. Arrange them in a large glass salad bowl. Grill the peppers on a baking tray lined with foil until they are blistered all over. Put into a plastic bag and seal. Set aside for 10 minutes to steam, (this makes them easier to skin). Remove the skin and seeds and cut the flesh into fine julienne strips. Arrange the strips over the salad and garnish with violets and tomatoes.

TO MAKE THE VINAIGRETTE: in a bowl whisk all the ingredients together. Drizzle the salad dressing over at the moment of serving. Do not toss the salad.

GREEN SALAD WITH BEAN SPROUTS

SERVES 6

1 mignonette lettuce
100 g/4 oz mung bean sprouts
50 g/2 oz alfalfa sprouts
1 tablespoon chopped celery leaves
1 tablespoon freshly chopped chives
120 ml/4 fl oz Basic Vinaigrette (see page
* 40)*

Wash the lettuce leaves, pat them dry and tear into small pieces. Place in a salad bowl with the sprouts, celery leaves and chives. Pour over the vinaigrette dressing. Toss lightly together and serve.

FEAST OF FLOWERS

Light salads benefit from the inclusion of edible flowers that provide colour and flavour as well as a touch of the unexpected. The recipes in this section include flowers of marrow, rose and violet, as well as leaves of nasturtium (the flowers may also be used). Many flowering plants, such as marigold, dandelion, tansy, bergamot and sweet Cicely, much used in medieval European kitchens, are now being revived where they are readily available. Food displayed on large, decorative leaves often looks even more tempting than on conventional china. Float borage flowers in long cooling drinks. Remember, choose additions of flowers, berries and leaves with care. The most colourful and attractive unfortunately often have the worst effects.

Fresh and golden, Green Salad with Rose Petals is an appetising side dish.

GREEN SALAD WITH ROSE PETALS

SERVES 6-8

1 large crisp lettuce
leaves from 1 bunch watercress
½ cucumber, peeled and sliced
1 chicory
100 g/4 oz mange tout, blanched,
*   refreshed and drained*

DRESSING:
4 tablespoons white wine or tarragon
*   vinegar*
2 teaspoons honey
120 ml/4 fl oz good-quality olive oil
salt
freshly ground black pepper
1-2 tablespoons freshly chopped mixed
*   herbs (such as thyme, marjoram, mint*
*   and parsley)*

GARNISH:
2 hard-boiled eggs, chopped
fresh petals from 1 yellow rose

Wash the lettuce leaves, pat them dry and tear into pieces. Wash and dry the watercress leaves. Place all the salad greens in a serving bowl and toss lightly.

TO MAKE THE DRESSING: place the vinegar in a small heavy saucepan and heat it over a very low heat for 1 minutes. Away from the heat, stir in the honey until it has melted. Place the sweetened vinegar in a screwtop jar with the oil, seasoning and herbs. Shake well to blend all the ingredients.

TO ASSEMBLE THE SALAD: pour the prepared dressing over the salad greens and toss lightly together.

TO GARNISH: sprinkle the egg over the salad and garnish with rose petals.

SALAD OF TOMATOES AND PURPLE BASIL

SERVES 6

1 kg/2 lb ripe, red, firm tomatoes
leaves from 1 small bunch purple basil
salt
freshly ground black pepper
½ clove garlic, peeled and crushed
175 ml/6 fl oz virgin olive oil or a strong,
* pure, refined olive oil*
2-3 tablespoons red wine vinegar

Skin the tomatoes by dipping them in boiling water for a few seconds: the skins will come away easily. Cut them into quarters and remove the cores. Place the tomatoes in a salad bowl.

Add the basil leaves to the bowl. Season well and sprinkle with garlic. Pour over the oil and toss carefully. Add vinegar to taste and toss carefully again. Serve at once.

COURGETTE FLOWER SALAD

SERVES 10

450 g/1 lb courgettes with flowers intact
1 tablespoon olive oil
1 large white or Spanish onion, peeled
* and sliced finely*
1 tablespoon freshly chopped marjoram
175 g/6 oz black olives, pitted
4 tablespoons lemon juice
salt
freshly ground black pepper

Steam the courgettes for 10 minutes until just tender. Leave to cool.

Heat the olive oil in a frying pan over a moderate heat and cook the onion until translucent. Remove from the pan and cool.

Toss the courgettes, onion, marjoram

and olives in a serving bowl with the lemon juice. Season with salt and pepper to taste. Chill in the refrigerator for 30 minutes before serving.

CUCUMBER AND YOGHURT SALAD

SERVES 4

1 large cucumber
350 ml/12 fl oz plain yoghurt
salt
freshly ground pepper
4-6 tablespoons chopped mint

GARNISH:
sprig of mint

Peel the cucumber and cut it in half lengthways. Hollow out the seeds with a teaspoon and slice the cucumber into 5 mm/¼ inch thick slices. Place in a bowl, cover and refrigerate until required.

Mix the cucumber with the yoghurt, season with salt and pepper to taste and mix in the chopped mint. Pile the salad into a serving dish and garnish with a sprig of mint.

CUCUMBER VINAIGRETTE

SERVES 6

24 very small continental cucumbers or
* gherkins, peeled and sliced*
salt
freshly ground black pepper
120 ml/4 fl oz Basic Vinaigrette (see page
* 40)*

Place the sliced cucumbers in a serving bowl. Season lightly with salt and pepper. Pour the vinaigrette over the cucumber, toss together and serve.

PEPPER SALAD WITH CAPERS

SERVES 8

1 tomato, chopped and drained
1 clove garlic, peeled and chopped
5 fresh basil leaves, torn into pieces
15 mint leaves
4 tablespoons olive oil
salt
freshly ground pepper
4 large sweet peppers, yellow, red and
* green combined, if possible*
1 litre/1¾ pints cold water
2 tablespoons capers, drained

GARNISH:
mint leaves

Place the tomato, garlic, basil and mint leaves in a bowl and pour over the olive oil. Season to taste and mix with a wooden spoon. Cover the bowl and refrigerate for 1 hour.

Place the peppers in a baking dish with the cold water and roast on the bottom shelf of a pre-heated, moderately hot oven 190°C/375°F, Gas Mark 5, for about 40 minutes, turning several times. Remove them from the oven, cool slightly and place in a plastic bag for 15 minutes. Remove them from the bag and rinse under cold water to cool. Peel and seed, carefully removing the white part, and cut into thin strips.

TO ASSEMBLE THE SALAD: pile the sliced peppers on to a serving dish, pour the tomato mixture over and refrigerate for at least 1 hour. Sprinkle with the capers just before serving and garnish with the mint leaves.

VIOLET PETAL AND TOMATO SALAD

SERVES 6

*1.5 kg/3 lb tomatoes, skinned, seeded and
 diced
2 tablespoons peeled and chopped shallots
2 tablespoons malt vinegar
40 g/1½ oz sultanas
40 g/1½ oz pecan nuts, chopped coarsely
120 ml/4 fl oz walnut oil
2 tablespoons Cointreau
salt
freshly ground black pepper
4 tablespoons violet petals*

Mix together the tomatoes, shallots and
malt vinegar. Leave to marinate for 20
minutes.

In another bowl, place the sultanas,
pecan nuts, walnut oil and Cointreau. Mix
and marinate for 20 minutes.

Toss both mixtures together and season
to taste. Spoon salad on to 6 individual
plates and scatter over the violet petals.
Serve the salad immediately.

ASSEMBLE WITH CARE

While the barbecue is sizzling, a selection
of salads will tempt your guests with
visual appeal. Choose ingredients to contrast and complement each other: bear in
mind not only colours – from creamy chicory to dark green watercress – and textures, whether firm carrots or smooth
avocado, but also shape (see, for
example, the salad on page 49).

Violet Petal and Tomato Salad is an intriguing blend of colours and textures.

VEGETABLE, FRUIT AND NUT SALAD

SERVES 8

225 g/8 oz young carrots, peeled and
* chopped finely*
1 small cucumber, chopped
4 celery stalks, chopped finely
225 g/8 oz baby courgettes, sliced finely
1 large sweet red pepper, peeled, seeded
* and cut into julienne*
1 large clove garlic, peeled and chopped
* finely*
1 tablespoon freshly chopped chives
2 sweet red apples, cored and sliced
1 banana, peeled and sliced
100 g/4 oz fresh dates, pitted and sliced
100 g/4 oz tiny cauliflower florets
1 tablespoon sunflower seeds
50 g/2 oz alfalfa sprouts
50 g/2 oz almonds, peeled and halved
50 g/2 oz cashew nuts
1 tablespoon sultanas
dried figs, apricots, peaches or pears, sliced
* very finely (optional)*

DRESSING:
120 ml/4 fl oz lemon juice
4 tablespoons honey
120 ml/4 fl oz extra virgin olive oil

TO MAKE THE DRESSING: place the lemon juice
in a small pan over a low heat. Add the
honey and stir for 1 minute. Remove the pan
from the heat and continue stirring until the
honey dissolves. Pour the sweetened lemon
juice into a screwtop jar, add the oil and
shake vigorously to blend.

TO ASSEMBLE THE SALAD: prepare the salad
ingredients just before serving. Everything
must be extremely fresh. Place all the ingredients in a large salad bowl and combine
them thoroughly but lightly to avoid bruis-
ing the fruits. Pour over the dressing and
serve immediately.

Ingredients at the peak of perfection make a Vegetable, Fruit and Nut Salad.

BALKAN SALAD

SERVES 6

1 cucumber, peeled and sliced
salt
1 large onion, peeled and sliced
2 tablespoons white wine vinegar
1 kg/2 lb tomatoes, peeled and sliced
1 medium sweet green pepper, seeded and
*   sliced finely*

DRESSING:
4 tablespoons olive or sunflower oil
1 tablespoon white wine vinegar
1 tablespoon water
½ teaspoon sugar
salt

GARNISH:
paprika (optional)

Place the cucumber in a shallow dish and sprinkle with salt. Leave for 1 hour in the refrigerator. Place the onions in a shallow dish and pour over the vinegar. Leave to marinate for 1 hour.

Arrange the slices of tomato and green pepper in a serving dish. Drain the cucumber slices and squeeze out the water with your hands. Add them to the dish. Remove the onion slices from the marinade and separate them into rings. Add to the other vegetables.

TO MAKE THE DRESSING: place all the ingredients in a screwtop jar and shake to blend them well.

TO ASSEMBLE THE SALAD: pour the dressing over the salad. Place in the refrigerator for 1 hour. Serve the salad with a dusting of paprika if desired.

WATERCRESS AND WALNUT SALAD

SERVES 6

1 large bunch watercress
225 g/8 oz walnut halves

DRESSING:
4 tablespoons walnut oil
3 tablespoons white wine vinegar
1 teaspoon green herbed mustard
1 tablespoon freshly chopped chives
freshly ground black pepper

Select leafy pieces of watercress, discarding any long sections of stalk. Break into 10 cm/4 inch long pieces. Wash and dry them thoroughly and arrange in a serving bowl. Combine with the walnuts.

TO MAKE THE DRESSING: place all the ingredients in a screwtop jar and shake well.

TO SERVE: toss the watercress and walnuts in vinaigrette dressing and serve immediately.

PECAN AND MUSHROOM SALAD

For a more pronounced flavour, the pecan nuts may be lightly toasted.

SERVES 6

100 g/4 oz button mushrooms, sliced
*   finely*
2-3 tablespoons Basic Vinaigrette (see
*   page 40)*
100 g/4 oz pecan nuts, chopped
2-3 stalks celery, chopped
2 tablespoons freshly chopped parsley
4 spring onions, chopped

Put the mushrooms in a salad bowl, sprinkle with the dressing and toss well. Add the remaining ingredients and combine them well. Chill for 1-2 hours.

SPINACH, PINE NUT AND MUSHROOM SALAD

SERVES 6

225 g/8 oz button mushrooms, quartered
120-175 ml/4-6 fl oz Basic Vinaigrette (see
*   page 40)*
1 bunch endive
1 head lettuce
450 g/1 lb tender young spinach leaves
2 tablespoons pine nuts, toasted
50 g/2 oz chopped spring onions
1 avocado, sliced (optional)

Marinate the button mushrooms in 120 ml/4 fl oz vinaigrette for 2 hours. Wash the endive, lettuce and spinach leaves and pat dry on a clean tea towel. Just before serving, tear the endive, lettuce and larger spinach leaves into pieces. Place all the salad greens in a bowl with the mushrooms and marinade. Add the pine nuts, spring onions and avocado if used. Toss together lightly but well and add more vinaigrette if necessary.

WELL-BEHAVED SALADS

For barbecues and other occasions when guests may not be seated when they eat, serve food that can easily be eaten with a fork or cut into bite-sized pieces. Peel thick skinned tomatoes by briefly scorching the skins or by dipping in boiling water after scoring the skin. . Remove stones from olives, and peel and clean prawns. Tear lettuce and other salad leaves . . . and provide plenty of table napkins!

CRISPY VEGETABLE SALAD

SERVES 6

*½ head medium cauliflower, trimmed
  and cut into florets*
*1 large bunch broccoli, trimmed and cut
  into florets*
*6 small carrots, peeled and cut in half
  lengthways*
225 g/8 oz baby squash, green or yellow
*175 g/6 oz mange tout, topped and
  stringed*
*any other seasonal vegetable of your
  choice*

DRESSING:
1 egg
2 teaspoons Dijon mustard
120 ml/4 fl oz tarragon vinegar
175 ml/6 fl oz vegetable oil
salt
freshly ground pepper

GARNISH:
finely chopped spring onions

Bring a large saucepan of salted water to the
boil and blanch the cauliflower and broccoli for 2 minutes only so that they are still
crisp. Refresh them in iced water and drain
them well. Repeat the process with the carrots and squash, cooking them until just tender. Drop the mange tout into boiling
water, drain immediately and refresh under
cold water.
TO MAKE THE DRESSING: whisk the egg with
the mustard and vinegar in a bowl. Whisk-
ing constantly, add all the oil slowly until in-
corporated. Season to taste.
TO SERVE: arrange all the vegetables in a
bowl. Spoon over the mayonnaise, sprinkle
with spring onions and serve at once.

SALAD OF TOMATO, PURPLE ONION AND AVOCADO

SERVES 8

*6 tomatoes, skinned, seeds removed and
  flesh cut in dice*
2 purple onions, peeled and cut in dice
2 firm avocados, peeled and cut in dice
3-4 sprigs fresh lemon thyme

VINAIGRETTE:
3 teaspoons whole seed mustard
freshly ground black pepper
1 tablespoon white wine vinegar
150 ml/¼ pints grape seed oil
salt to taste

Put the tomatoes, onions and avocados in a
serving bowl with the leaves and thyme.
    Place all the ingredients for the vinai-
grette in a screwtop jar and shake well. Toss
the salad with enough vinaigrette to moisten. Taste for seasoning and serve at once.

AVOCADO, BEAN SHOOT AND OLIVE SALAD

SERVES 6

*3 small just-ripe avocados, peeled and
  sliced*
175 g/6 oz stuffed olives, sliced
250 g/9 oz bean shoots
2 spring onions, sliced finely
*120-175 ml/4-6 fl oz Basic Vinaigrette (see
  page 40)*
salt and freshly ground black pepper

Place the avocados in a salad bowl with the
stuffed olives, bean shoots and spring
onions. Toss lightly with the vinaigrette
dressing, adding a little more salt and pepper if needed. Serve at once.

AUSTRALIA SALAD

SERVES 8

1 cos lettuce
1 mignonette lettuce
1 endive
4 kiwi fruit, peeled and cut in slices
2 bananas, peeled and cut in slices
*1 small white radish (daikon), peeled and
  cut in batons*
250 ml/8 fl oz Basic Vinaigrette (page 40)

Wash and drain the lettuce and endive and
tear them in small pieces into a salad bowl.
Add the kiwi fruit, bananas and radish. Toss
with vinaigrette. Serve immediately.

SALADE VERTE

SERVES 6-8

12 young chicory
1 mignonette lettuce
½ head endive
*2 firm, ripe, green pears, peeled, cored
  and sliced*
*1 large, ripe avocado, peeled, halved and
  sliced*
12 green olives, pitted
50 g/2 oz alfalfa sprouts
2 tablespoons finely chopped parsley

DRESSING:
6 tablespoons olive oil
2 tablespoons white wine vinegar
½ teaspoon dry mustard
salt
freshly ground black pepper
1 teaspoon sugar
1 tablespoon finely chopped shallots

Wash the chicory, lettuce and endive very
well. Drain well to prevent any moisture

diluting the dressing. Tear the leaves into bite-sized pieces and place in a large salad bowl.

Add the pears and avocado slices to the salad bowl. Toss in the olives, alfalfa sprouts and parsley.

Whisk all the dressing ingredients together or shake well to blend in a screwtop jar. Pour over the salad and toss gently, but enough to coat everything well. Serve immediately.

POTATO SALAD

Make a day before use.

SERVES 10

6-8 large potatoes, unpeeled
4 medium white onions, peeled and sliced
parsley, chopped finely
salt
freshly ground pepper
2 teaspoons sugar
175 ml/6 fl oz white vinegar
a little olive oil
120-175 ml/4-6 fl oz boiling water

Oyster Mushroom, Avocado and Nut Salad is appetising and attractive.

Boil the potatoes in salted water until soft. Peel and slice them coarsely while they are as hot as you can handle. Put a layer of potatoes in a large mixing bowl, then a layer of onions, then a layer of chopped parsley. Sprinkle with salt, fresh ground pepper and sugar. Repeat these layers until all the ingredients are used. Pour the vinegar over the bowl (the potatoes should still be quite hot), and add the olive oil sparingly. Finally, add a good dash of boiling water. Toss the salad immediately with two large spoons, being careful not to break the potato more than you can help. Leave to cool and toss the salad again 4-5 times before serving.

OYSTER MUSHROOM, AVOCADO AND NUT SALAD

SERVES 6

450 g/1 lb runner beans or French beans
100 g/4 oz button mushrooms, sliced
finely
50 g/2 oz pecan nuts or pepita nuts
salt and freshly ground black pepper
120 ml/4 fl oz Basic Vinaigrette (page 40)
200 g/7 oz oyster mushrooms
6 cooked baby artichokes
1 sweet red pepper, cut in julienne
2 avocados, peeled, halved and sliced

Cut the beans in 132 cm/5 inch lengths and cook in boiling salted water until just tender. Rinse immediately under cold water and drain. Place in a bowl with the sliced mushrooms, pecan nuts, salt and pepper to taste and a little vinaigrette. Stir gently to combine then transfer to the centre of a shallow serving dish. Arrange the oyster mushrooms, artichokes and pepper around the edge, with the slices of avocado across the centre. Drizzle the remaining vinaigrette over the salad and serve.

SALAD OF WALNUTS AND ROQUEFORT CHEESE

SERVES 4

1 cos lettuce
12 small rounds of bread
100 g/4 oz unsalted butter
100 g /4 oz Roquefort cheese

VINAIGRETTE:
2 tablespoons cider vinegar
1 teaspoon Dijon mustard
6 tablespoons walnut oil
salt
pepper

GARNISH:
20 walnut halves
fresh herbs

Use only the young, crisp leaves from the centre of the lettuce. Wash them well and pat dry on a tea towel.

Heat the oven to moderately hot, 200°C/400°F, Gas Mark 6. Spread the bread rounds with a little butter and bake in the oven for 10 minutes or until they are golden brown. Set them aside.

Mash the cheese and remaining butter together in a bowl and spread it on the cold croûtons.

TO MAKE THE VINAIGRETTE: place all the ingredients in a screwtop jar and shake well to amalgamate.

TO SERVE THE SALAD: arrange the lettuce leaves on individual salad plates and pour over the vinaigrette. Scatter the prepared croûtons over the salad and garnish with walnut pieces and fresh herbs. Serve the salad at once.

Fresh herbs in season garnish a Salad of Walnuts and Roquefort Cheese.

TOMATO AND BOCCONCINO SALAD

SERVES 4

*1 medium, fresh bocconcino cheese or 175
  g/6 oz mozzarella
450 g/1 lb cherry tomatoes or 4 medium
  tomatoes
a few sprigs of basil
salt and freshly ground pepper
120 ml/4 fl oz Basic Vinaigrette (page 40)*

Cut the cheese into thin slices and arrange them around the edge of a serving plate. Cut the cherry tomatoes in half or slice the larger tomatoes and pile them in the centre of the serving plate.

Tear the basil leaves and sprinkle them over the tomatoes, adding salt and pepper to taste. Drizzle the vinaigrette over the tomatoes. Serve immediately.

POTATO SALAD WITH TARRAGON MAYONNAISE

SERVES 6

8 medium new potatoes, unpeeled

DRESSING:
*1 egg
½ tablespoon tarragon wine vinegar
175 ml/6 fl oz olive oil
250 ml/8 fl oz soya bean oil
2-3 tablespoons freshly chopped tarragon
salt and freshly ground black pepper*

GARNISH:
*1 sweet red pepper, sliced
calamatta olives, pitted and halved
sprigs of fresh tarragon*

Bring a saucepan of salted water to the boil. Add the potatoes and boil steadily until they are cooked but not soft. Drain. As soon as they can be handled, peel them and allow to cool. Cut lengthways and slice diagonally. Arrange the slices in a serving bowl.

TO MAKE THE DRESSING: place the egg in a blender or food processor with a few drops of vinegar. Process briefly. With the motor running, add the oils alternately in a thin but steady stream, occasionally adding a few drops of the remaining vinegar until none is left. Finally stir in the tarragon and season.

TO SERVE: pour the mayonnaise over the potatoes. Garnish with slices of red pepper, olives and sprigs of tarragon, and serve.

CHERRY TOMATOES STUFFED WITH AVOCADO

SERVES 6

*750 g/1½ lb cherry tomatoes
salt
freshly ground black pepper
1 tablespoon sugar
2 ripe avocados, peeled and halved
2 tablespoons soured cream
4 teaspoons lime juice
4 teaspoons lemon juice
3 tablespoons finely chopped parsley and
  chives
Tabasco sauce*

Cut thin slices from the tops of the tomatoes. Remove the seeds and pulp with a small melon ball scooper. Sprinkle the tomato shells with salt, pepper and sugar and invert on a plate lined with paper towels to drain.

Mash the avocados in a bowl and combine them with the cream, citrus juices and herbs. Season with Tabasco and add black pepper to taste.

Fill the tomatoes with the avocado purée. Chill for 30 minutes before serving.

CUCUMBER STUFFED WITH HERB CHEESE

MAKES 60 BITE-SIZED PIECES

*350 g/12 oz cream cheese
4-6 tablespoons freshly chopped mixed
  herbs (such as parsley, chives, French
  tarragon, oregano, thyme, rosemary
  and garlic, or a mixture of green
  peppercorns and mint)
1 large cucumber
salt
freshly ground black pepper*

Spoon the cream cheese into a bowl and beat it well to soften it. Stir in the mixed herbs a little at a time until they are thoroughly combined. Cover the bowl and leave in a cool place for up to 24 hours for the flavours to develop.

Peel the cucumber and cut it in half lengthways. Scoop out the seeds. Sprinkle salt over the cucumber and leave for 30 minutes. Drain and pat dry thoroughly with paper towels.

Fill the cucumber with the herb cheese. Dust lightly with pepper. Cut into pieces 2.5 cm/1 inch long and arrange them on a flat dish. Serve immediately.

STUFFED VEGETABLES

Rice-based stuffings flavoured with prawns, chopped chicken, flaked smoked fish, herbs, nuts, diced ham or sausage are excellent ways of filling many types of fresh vegetables.

MAIN COURSE SALADS

THAI SALAD

SERVES 4

175 g/6 oz cabbage, shredded
2 small carrots, peeled and grated
5 tablespoons roasted unsalted peanuts,
    crushed coarsely
50 g/2 oz ground dried shrimps
1 tablespoon chilli sauce
2 small tomatoes, chopped roughly

DRESSING:
3 tablespoons nam pla (fish sauce)
2 teaspoons sugar
freshly ground black pepper
3 cloves garlic, peeled and crushed
4 tablespoons lemon juice

Put all the salad ingredients in a bowl and
toss them together.

To make the dressing, place all the ingredients in a screwtop jar and shake well.

Pour the dressing over the salad and turn
the ingredients over with 2 wooden spoons
to coat them evenly. Refrigerate the salad
and serve cold.

PRAWN AND MANGO SALAD

SERVES 6

1 large mango, peeled
1 kg/2 lb cooked medium Mediterranean
    prawns
salt and freshly ground black pepper
juice of 1-2 limes

GARNISH:
coriander leaves

Slice the mango into 6 even slices and
arrange them around a serving plate. Peel
and clean the prawns but leave on the tails.
Place them in the centre of the plate.

Sprinkle salt and pepper over the
prawns. Drizzle over the lime juice. Scatter
with coriander leaves and serve the salad
lightly chilled.

SALADE NIÇOISE

SERVES 8

1 head crisp lettuce
3×200 g/7 oz cans tuna, drained
    and broken into chunks
1 kg/2 lb cherry tomatoes, whole or
    halved
225 g/8 oz pitted black olives
1 large Spanish onion, peeled and
    sliced thinly or 6 spring onions,
    chopped
1 large sweet green pepper, cut in strips
1 large sweet red pepper, cut in
    strips
6 hard-boiled eggs, quartered
2×50 g/2 oz cans anchovies, in strips
    or rolled around capers
2 tablespoons freshly chopped parsley

GARLIC DRESSING:
1 tablespoon dry mustard
1 tablespoon sea salt
1 teaspoon sugar
freshly ground black pepper
2 cloves garlic, peeled and crushed
120 ml/4 fl oz tarragon vinegar
4 tablespoons lemon juice
500 ml/18 fl oz olive oil

Separate the lettuce leaves and use them to
line a large salad bowl. Place the tuna
chunks in the centre, and arrange the tomatoes, olives, onion, peppers, eggs and
anchovies around them. Add a sprinkling of
parsley.

TO MAKE THE DRESSING: combine the mustard, salt, sugar, a few good grinds of pepper
and garlic in a mixing bowl. Whisk in the
vinegar and lemon juice. Finally whisk in
the olive oil, stirring vigorously to amalgamate the ingredients.

TO SERVE: pour half the dressing over the
salad and serve the remainder separately in
a sauceboat.

TUNA FISH AND GREEN BEAN SALAD

SERVES 8

450 g/1 lb green beans, topped and
    tailed
4 tablespoons olive oil
1×200 g/7 oz can tuna, drained
8 tablespoons black olives, pitted
225 g/8 oz cherry tomatoes
4 hard-boiled eggs, quartered

GARNISH:
1 bunch Italian parsley, chopped
freshly ground black pepper

Steam the whole beans for 5-10 minutes
until they are just tender. Refresh them
under cold water so that they retain their
bright colour. Arrange the whole beans in a
serving dish, pour the olive oil over them
and chill.

When ready to serve the salad, shred the
tuna over the beans and arrange the olives,
tomatoes and eggs on top. Garnish with the
Italian parsley and freshly ground black
pepper.

CRAB SALAD

SERVES 8

225g/8 oz fresh crab meat
2 stalks celery, chopped
salt
freshly ground black pepper

MAYONNAISE:
3 egg yolks
juice of ½ lemon
salt
freshly ground black pepper
1 teaspoon Dijon mustard
a little garlic juice (optional)
175 ml/6 fl oz peanut oil
175 ml/6 fl oz olive oil
1 tablespoon boiling water
2 tablespoons single cream

GARNISH:
8 small ripe red tomatoes cut in
  eighths
2-3 leaves chicory

TO MAKE THE MAYONNAISE: put the egg yolks in the bowl of a blender or food processor with the lemon juice, salt and pepper, mustard and garlic juice and process well. Mix the 2 oils together in a jug. With the motor running, add the oil gradually until the mayonnaise thickens. Finally pour in the boiling water.

Transfer the mayonnaise to a bowl. When it is quite cold, mix in the cream. Taste to see if more lemon juice is required.

TO ASSEMBLE THE SALAD: add the crab meat and celery to the mayonnaise. Combine well and season with salt and pepper.

Place the tomato pieces around the edge of a serving plate like the petals of a flower. Spoon the crab mayonnaise into the centre and garnish on one side with chicory leaves.

A trio of enticing dishes from Italy. Clockwise from top: Tomato and Bocconcino Salad (see page 51), Pepper Salad with Capers (see page 44) and Tuna Fish and Green Bean Salad combine colourfully to make an irresistible mixture of Mediterranean flavours.

CHICKEN AND HONEYDEW MELON SALAD

SERVES 6

6 chicken fillets
250 ml/8 fl oz white wine
1 teaspoon black peppercorns
leaves from 2 celery stalks
2 stalks celery, chopped finely
4 tablespoons parsley, chopped finely
¼ large honeydew melon, peeled, seeded
    and sliced

GINGER MAYONNAISE:
150 ml/¼ pint Classic Mayonnaise (see
    page 41)
150 ml/¼ pint soured cream
grated rind of 1 small lemon
4 tablespoons lemon juice
2 teaspoons honey
7.5 cm/3 inch piece green ginger, peeled
    and grated
salt and freshly ground black pepper

Chicken and Honeydew Melon Salad.

Place the chicken in a medium saucepan with the wine, peppercorns and celery leaves. Add just enough water to cover and poach gently until the chicken is tender.

Remove the chicken from the stock and cut it diagonally into bite-sized pieces. Leave to cool. Place the chicken pieces in a bowl with the celery stalks and parsley. Cut up the melon and add it to the bowl.

TO MAKE THE GINGER MAYONNAISE: blend the mayonnaise with the soured cream, lemon rind, lemon juice and honey. Add the ginger and season with salt and pepper to taste. Spoon the mayonnaise over and garnish with extra parsley.

CHICKEN WITH WATER CHESTNUTS AND WHITE GRAPES

SERVES 9-10

1 chicken (weighing 1.8 kg /3 lb 12 oz),
    steamed
1×225 g/8 oz can water chestnuts, diced
225 g/8 oz seedless white grapes, washed
3 stalks celery, chopped finely
100 g/4 oz slivered almonds, toasted
250 ml/8 fl oz Classic Mayonnaise (see
    page 41)
120 ml/4 fl oz cream, whipped
½ tablespoon curry powder
1 tablespoon soy sauce
about 10 whole crisp lettuce leaves, to
    serve the salad

Remove the meat and skin from the chicken while it is still warm and cut into small pieces. Add the water chestnuts to the chicken. Pick the grapes from the stems and add them to the chicken and chestnuts with the celery and half the toasted almonds.

Combine the mayonnaise in a bowl with the cream, curry powder and soy sauce, and add to the chicken mixture. Mix well and season with salt and pepper to taste. Chill for 2-3 hours.

Using the lettuce leaves as containers, spoon in the chicken mixture, sprinkle the remaining nuts on top and serve.

SALAD OF SMOKED QUAIL AND PEACH WITH BASIL VINAIGRETTE

SERVES 4

VINAIGRETTE:
¼ bunch basil, leaves only, shredded
250 ml/8 fl oz olive oil
250 ml/8 fl oz peanut oil
120 ml/4 fl oz white wine vinegar
salt and freshly ground white pepper
½ teaspoon sugar
1 tablespoon lemon juice

SALAD:
1 small radicchio
½ cos lettuce
1 endive
½ bunch watercress
4 smoked quail, deboned and divided
    into sections
2 peaches, peeled and sliced
20 fresh basil leaves
8 quail eggs, hard-boiled and shelled

TO MAKE THE VINAIGRETTE: place all the ingredients in a screwtop jar and shake well until they are combined.

TO ASSEMBLE THE SALAD: arrange the leaves of radicchio, lettuce, endive and watercress on 4 salad plates. Place the pieces of quail on top and surround them with peach slices, basil leaves and quail eggs. Dress with the basil vinaigrette and serve immediately.

(Right) *Salad of Smoked Quail and*
Peach with Basil Vinaigrette.

'GLEN ELGIN' SALAD

SERVES 8

1 mignonette lettuce
1 cos lettuce
1 iceberg lettuce
1 bunch watercress
450 g/1 lb cherry tomatoes
3 eggs

225 g/8 oz bacon rashers, rind removed
9 slices bread
40 g/1½ oz butter

DRESSING:
1 tablespoon French mustard
1 clove garlic, peeled and crushed
salt
freshly ground white pepper
4 tablespoons white vinegar

1 tablespoon red wine vinegar
175 ml/6 fl oz olive oil
2 teaspoons sugar

GARNISH:
watercress sprigs

Wash, trim and prepare the salad ingredients ready to make the salad. Hard-boil the eggs, peel them and when they are cool

Croûtons and diced bacon give 'Glen Elgin' Salad extra crispness and bite.

press them through a sieve. Cut the bacon into small dice and fry it in its own fat until crisp. Drain it on paper towels and allow to cool. Cut the bread into small cubes to make croûtons. Heat the butter and fry the bread cubes until golden brown. Drain the croûtons well on paper towels and allow them to cool.

TO ASSEMBLE THE SALAD: arrange the lettuce and watercress on 8 plates, then add the whole baby tomatoes, sieved eggs, bacon pieces and croûtons.

TO MAKE THE DRESSING: place all the ingredients in a screwtop jar and shake until well blended.

TO FINISH THE SALAD: carefully spoon the dressing over each salad just before serving. Garnish with watercress sprigs.

DUCK AND ORANGE SALAD

SERVES 6-8

1 duck (weighing about 2 kg/4 lb)
200 g/7 oz runner beans or French beans
  topped and tailed
225 g/8 oz cauliflower or broccoli florets
oil for frying
50 g/2 oz almonds, peeled and sliced
1 small onion, peeled and chopped
  finely
3 stalks celery, sliced
salt
freshly ground pepper
200 g/7 oz bean sprouts
1 orange, peeled and sliced horizontally

DRESSING:
1 tablespoon sesame oil
1 tablespoon oyster sauce
2 tablespoons soy sauce
2 teaspoons sugar
2 teaspoons grated fresh ginger

Heat the oven to moderately hot, 190°C/375°F, Gas Mark 5. Place the duck on a wire rack in a roasting pan. Prick the skin all over with a fork and bake in the oven for 1¼ hours. When cold remove the flesh, discarding the skin, and cut it into 4 cm/1½ inch pieces.

Cut the beans into 5 cm/2 inch pieces. Drop the cauliflower or broccoli into a large saucepan of boiling salted water and blanch for about 3-4 minutes. Drain, refresh under cold water and drain again. Repeat this process with the beans.

Heat a little oil in a small pan over a moderate heat. Fry the almonds until nicely browned and drain.

TO MAKE THE DRESSING: place all the ingredients in a screwtop jar and shake well.

TO ASSEMBLE THE SALAD: place the cauliflower or broccoli, beans, onions and celery in a bowl and add the dressing. Toss well. Add the pieces of duck to the salad and toss again. Just before serving, taste for salt and pepper and add the bean sprouts. Arrange the orange slices on top and sprinkle with the browned almonds.

BEEF SALAD

SERVES 4

750 g/1½ lb porterhouse steak
2 cloves garlic
leaves from 2 coriander sprigs, chopped
¾ teaspoon sugar
2 teaspoons light soy sauce
2 teaspoons lemon juice
2 teaspoons nam pla (fish sauce)
freshly ground black pepper
2 bulbs spring onions, sliced finely
2 bulbs lemon grass, chopped finely
6 fresh red chillies, sliced finely
3 teaspoons roughly chopped mint
1 teaspoon roughly chopped parsley

Place the beef under a pre-heated hot grill and cook it to medium rare. Slice it into thin even pieces.

Crush the garlic into a large salad bowl. Add most of the chopped coriander leaves, sugar, soy sauce, lemon juice, nam pla and black pepper. Combine these ingredients well and add the spring onions, lemon grass and chillies. Toss together and mix in the slivers of beef. Just before serving, sprinkle with chopped mint, parsley and the remaining coriander leaves.

BACON AND SPINACH SALAD USA

SERVES 6

6 spring onions, cut diagonally in 2.5
  cm/1 inch pieces
6 hard-boiled eggs, sliced
6 rashers of bacon, cooked until crisp and
  crumbled
200 g/7 oz mushrooms, sliced through
  caps and stalks
leaves of 1 bunch spinach, washed and
  drained

DRESSING:
5 tablespoons red wine vinegar
250 ml/8 fl oz virgin olive oil
2 tablespoons French mustard (Dijon or
  coarsely-crushed mustard seed type)

Place the onions, eggs, bacon and mushrooms in a salad bowl.

TO MAKE THE DRESSING: place all the ingredients in a screwtop jar and shake well to amalgamate them.

TO SERVE: pour the dressing into the bowl and toss well but lightly. Add the spinach leaves just before serving, and toss again.

PICNICS

Pâtés, cold meats, pies and cakes
– a moveable feast for those long, lazy days

Picnics need even more careful planning than barbecues. Food naturally takes on a special importance because everyone seems to eat more when they are out of doors.

It is important that picnic foods are as interesting and as appetising as possible. The most casual affair need not necessarily be sandwich-oriented, although inventive sandwiches and rolls can prove sensational, especially when the bread is home-made. The food should be easy to eat and, above all, simple to transport. Pies, pâtés and terrines, and cold meats (often with an innovative filling) should form the basis. If you have a portable barbecue or are spending a day at a site where a barbecue is available, see pages 12-31 for ideas. A selection of seasonal salads and interesting dressings – added at the picnic, never before – can be followed by finger food such as fresh fruit, home-made cakes and biscuits, all easy to prepare and simple to handle.

Pack the food carefully, using small containers for cooked meats, salads and cheese. Food that breaks easily – quiches, pizzas, flans and so on – should be carried in cake containers or firm polythene boxes with lids. Make sure that the food remains upright for the journey, no matter how short. Transport is so much easier if you have a supply of insulated bags and boxes, packed with pre-frozen cooler bricks or sachets to keep food cold and fresh for hours – essential in hot summer weather.

For carrying liquids, invest in a range of vacuum flasks: conventional designs for traditional hot drinks, wide-mouthed jars to

Nature provides the setting for a picnic made perfect by all that's needed for pleasure and comfort — what better way to laze away a sunny summer's afternoon than in the shade of a tree with plentiful provisions?

59

For carrying liquids, invest in a range of vacuum flasks: conventional designs for traditional hot drinks, wide-mouthed jars to hold soups and casseroles for winter picnics. Remember that eight hours is the maximum time for liquids to remain hot or cold in a vacuum container.

Our love of the outdoors has led to a whole industry based on alfresco eating, producing linens and tableware, picnic baskets and portable coolers, which all travel happily to the beach or the park, go sailing or touring with equal flair, and look fashionably chic at either polo or the races (see right).

For warm-weather picnics you may like to invest in a wine cooler like this one. Made of terracotta, it will keep wine crisp and chilled.

The comfort of your guests should be of equal consideration to the food. You may be picnicking where there are seats and tables provided, but take along folding chairs, at least for older members of the party, a supply of cushions and rugs, and sturdy folding tables on which to set out drinks as well as the picnic proper. And be prepared for sudden showers! A supply of large umbrellas will shelter you all from rain as well as afford protection from the sun. You may also like to provide a small 'crisis kit', containing insect repellent, sunscreen creams, sun hats and a basic first-aid kit with bandages, plasters, anti-sting creams and the like.

If children are invited along, be sure to include plenty of books, toys and games to keep them amused, plus bags for their inevitable souvenirs – seashells, pebbles and the like. Take a supply of towels, wet towelling cloths and tissues – as well as being invaluable when children are around they will enable you to cope with muddy dogs, spills and disasters of many kinds.

Always obey the country code and remember to pack rubbish bags. A little forward planning can save a lot of trouble and embarrassment on the day.

A wicker basket for carrying bottles is a stylish partner to your picnic hamper – practical, attractive and effective.

Plates and cups

Unbreakable plates and saucers are strapped neatly to the lid of the picnic hamper, and cups can stack inside each other to fit snugly between food containers and vacuum flasks.

Vacuum flasks

Invaluable for picnics, these ensure warming drinks and soups for cold weather outings, and deliciously chilled refreshments for hot summer days. Liquids will stay hot or cold for 8 hours.

Cutlery

Choose tough, unbreakable cutlery which can then travel to the picnic strapped to the hamper lid. This is secured to the base with a small chain to stop the whole thing tipping over when it is opened.

Food containers

You will always need an array of airtight containers of all shapes and sizes to accommodate salads, sauces and dressings, cold meats, picnic bakes, cakes and biscuits, condiments and so on.

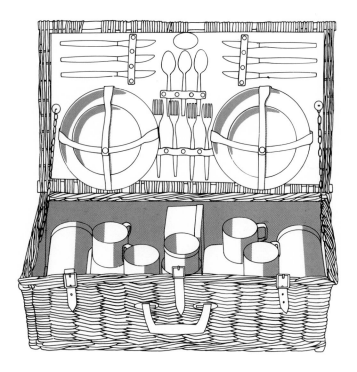

THE WELL-EQUIPPED PICNIC HAMPER

Above you will find a picnic hamper which contains all the essentials for stylish and comfortable picnicking. You can either buy a hamper which is already equipped or start with an empty one and build it up gradually to suit your individual needs. Cutlery should be efficient – nothing is more irritating than plastic knives and forks which have an uncanny knack of snapping whenever they are within striking distance of food – and reasonably inexpensive. Perhaps you will opt for a cheerful design with coloured handles matched to linen or tableware to create a

lighthearted mood. Plates, cups and saucers should also be unbreakable. With all these items you will find plenty of designs to choose from; these may often be inexpensive yet the best still retain a great sense of style.

You will also need a collection of unbreakable lidded containers to transport salads and bakes, unbreakable screw-top jars for salad dressings, and an assortment of small containers for salt, pepper and sugar.

For cooler days invest in a selection of mugs with lids to hold warming soups,

often a meal in themselves. Two or three vacuum flasks for hot or cold drinks are essentials and you will also need insulated carrying bags or boxes to take anything which should be served chilled to the picnic. Last but not least, make provision for transporting drinks and keeping them cool (see left).

Include a tablecloth with matching napkins in your picnic paraphernalia. Be imaginative and choose colours and designs to suit the setting, such as flowered cottons for the countryside, practical towelling for the beach.

PICNIC CHECKLIST

- **Food:** all courses, plus basics such as bread, butter, salt, pepper, dressings in screwtop jars.
- **Drinks:** wine, beers, fruit juices, mineral water. Tea and coffee in vacuum flasks, a large bottle of fresh water to make tea. A kettle for doing just that. Wine cooler, cooler blocks.
- **Picnic setting:** tableware in firm plastic or unbreakable china; good-looking, inexpensive glasses and cutlery; tablecloths and napkins – inexpensive fabric rather than paper.
- **Flat-bottomed baskets:** to carry items that don't need refrigeration. They will double as trays for bread and cheeses, and salad selections.
- **Cooking:** if it's a barbecue picnic, take dry wood (it's *always* wet on site), matches, fire starters and newspaper, grill or wire to hold meat, pans. Make sure that fires are permitted at your chosen site.
- **Protection:** big umbrellas for shelter from sun and showers; insect repellent; sunscreen creams; extra sun hats; basic first-aid kit which should include anti-sting treatment.
- **Children:** amusements such as bats, balls, fishing lines; a spare outfit per child; plenty of towels and wet towelling cloths (these will be invaluable anyway); extra tissues.
- **Most-forgotten items:** a sharp knife (wrap it in several layers of newspaper), corkscrew, bottle and can openers, matches, bag to take home rubbish.

BREADS & SCONES FOR PICNICS

WHITE BREAD DOUGH

MAKES 2 LOAVES OR 30 ROLLS

875 g/1¾ lb strong unbleached flour
12 g/scant ½ oz salt
20 g/scant 1 oz fresh yeast
½ tablespoon sugar
1 teaspoon malt extract
500 ml/18 fl oz milk
1-2 tablespoons sesame or poppy seeds (optional)

Sift the flour and salt together into a large bowl. Blend the yeast in a small bowl with the sugar, malt and 150 ml/¼ pint milk. Make a well in the centre of the flour and pour in the yeast liquid with the remaining milk. Mix all together with one hand to make a dough, working until the dough comes away cleanly from the sides of the bowl. Turn the ball of dough out on to a floured surface and knead it well. Place into a greased bowl, cover and leave to rest in a warm place for 1-1½ hours or until double in bulk. Knock down the risen dough to bring it back to its original size. Let it rise again for another hour. Knead it again and let it rest for 10 minutes.

Heat the oven to moderately hot, 200°C/400°F, Gas Mark 6.

Form the dough into rolls on a baking sheet or loaves in 450 g/1 lb tins. Leave to prove, covered with cling film or a tea towel to prevent them from drying out, for 10-15 minutes. For seeded rolls or loaves, brush the tops lightly with salted water and sprinkle over the seeds.

Bake the loaves in the oven for about 40 minutes. Turn off the heat and leave for about 20 minutes longer. The loaves should sound hollow when tapped on the bottom. Bake rolls in the oven for 20 minutes. Leave loaves and rolls to cool on a wire rack.

WALNUT BREAD

MAKES 1 × 500 g/1¼ lb LOAF

20 g/scant 1 oz fresh yeast
1 tablespoon golden syrup
500 ml/18 fl oz warm water
285 g/10½ oz wholemeal flour
285 g/10½ oz strong flour (made from durum wheat)
1 teaspoon salt
150 g/5 oz walnuts, chopped coarsely
1½ tablespoons walnut oil
50 g/2 oz onion, chopped finely

Mix the yeast and syrup with enough warm water to give a creamy consistency. Sift the flours with the salt and make a well in the middle. Pour in the yeast mixture and remaining water, mixing them in with one hand while adding the nuts, oil and onion with the other. Mix well until the ball of dough comes away cleanly from the sides of the bowl. Turn the dough out on to a floured board and knead well. Place the ball of dough in an oiled bowl and cover with a cloth, or in an oiled plastic bag. Leave until doubled in bulk. Knock back the dough and shape it into an oiled baking tin. Heat the oven to hot, 220°C/425°F, Gas Mark 7. Leave the dough in a warm place, covered, for 30 minutes until well risen.

Bake for 45 minutes. Turn the heat off, remove the loaf from the tin and leave in the oven for 5 minutes to crisp. Cool on a rack.

No picnic is complete without a basketful of fresh home-made bread and rolls to accompany the food and drinks.

WHOLEMEAL BREAD

MAKES 1×1 KG/2 LB LOAF AND 12 ROLLS

1 kg/2 lb plain flour
1 teaspoon salt
450 g/1 lb wholemeal flour
40 g/1½ oz fresh yeast
40 g/1½ oz sugar
750 ml/1¼ pints warm water
50 g/2 oz margarine

Sift the plain flour and salt and mix in the wholemeal flour. Combine the yeast and sugar with ⅓ of the water and leave to activate. Work the margarine into the flour with your fingertips. Add the frothy yeast and remaining water and work into the mixture. Knead for about 10 minutes until no longer sticky. Cover and leave to rise in a warm place until doubled in bulk. Knock back and reknead until firm. Shape ⅔ to fit a large greased loaf tin; shape the rest into 12 rolls and place on a baking sheet. Leave to rise. Bake at 230°C/450°F, Gas Mark 8 for about 10-15 minutes (rolls) and 45 minutes (loaf).

PARMESAN HERB BREAD

MAKES 3 SMALL LOAVES

275 g/10 oz plain flour
1¼ teaspoons salt
½ teaspoon bicarbonate of soda
2 teaspoons baking powder
⅛ teaspoon cayenne
1 teaspoon dried sage, crumbled
1 teaspoon coarsely ground pepper
100 g/4 oz freshly grated Parmesan cheese
25 g/1 oz minced fresh parsley leaves
50 g/2 oz solid margarine, softened
2 tablespoons sugar
2 large eggs, beaten lightly
300 ml/½ pint buttermilk
½ teaspoon Worcestershire sauce

Heat the oven to moderate, 180°C/350°F, Gas mark 4. In a bowl combine well with a fork the flour, salt, bicarbonate of soda, baking powder, cayenne, sage, pepper, Parmesan cheese and parsley. In a large bowl, stir together the margarine and sugar, add the eggs and combine the mixture well. Stir in the buttermilk and Worcestershire sauce, mixing well. Add the flour mixture and stir in the batter until it is just combined. Divide the batter between 3 greased loaf tins, measuring 14 × 7.5 × 5 cm/5½ × 3⅛ × 2¼ inches and bake in the middle of the oven for 40-50 minutes or until a skewer comes out clean. Let the loaves cool in the tins on a rack for 10 minutes. Loosen the edges with a knife, turn the loaves right side up onto the rack, and let them cool for 2 hours.

The bread keeps, wrapped in foil and chilled, for up to 5 days, or it may be frozen.

PANE DI ROMARINO

(Rosemary Bread)

MAKES 1 LOAF

25 g/1 oz fresh yeast
scant 250 ml/8 fl oz warm water
375 g/13 oz plain flour
100 g/4 oz raisins
120 ml/4 fl oz olive oil
2 heaped tablespoons fresh rosemary
* leaves*
pinch of salt

In a bowl mix the yeast with 5 tablespoons of warm water and 75 g/3 oz flour. Leave in a warm place until the mixture starts to bubble. Soak the raisins in cold water for 20 minutes. Drain. Heat the olive oil in a small pan over a moderate heat and add 1 tablespoon rosemary. Cook until the leaves turn lightly brown. Set the pan aside to cool.

When the yeast is frothy, stir in all the rosemary in oil. Add the drained raisins, salt and remaining warm water. Mix well. Add the uncooked rosemary. Work in the remaining flour, little by little, until you have a smooth dough. Turn out on to a floured surface. Knead for about 10 minutes.

Heat the oven to hot, 220°C/425°F, Gas Mark 7. Place the dough in an oiled 20 cm/8 inch spring-release tin. Cover with a tea towel and leave to rise in a warm place until doubled in bulk. Bake in the oven for 40-50 minutes. Remove from the oven, release the tin and leave to cool. Serve warm or cold.

BABY CHEESE SCONES

MAKES ABOUT 20

225 g/8 oz self-raising flour
¼ teaspoon dry mustard
pinch salt
generous pinch cayenne
25 g/1 oz butter
65 g/2½ oz sharp cheese, grated
1 egg, beaten
120-175 ml/4-6 fl oz milk

Into a large mixing bowl sift together the flour, mustard, salt and cayenne. Rub in the butter and cheese. Combine the beaten egg and 120 ml/4 fl oz milk and gradually blend the liquid in to form a dough. Be careful that the dough is neither too dry nor too wet. It may be necessary to add a little more milk. Transfer the dough to a floured surface, roll it out to 1 cm/½ inch thick and cut out the scones with a 4 cm/1½ inch cutter.

Heat the oven to moderately hot, 200°C/400°F, Gas Mark 6. Place the scones on a lightly oiled baking sheet. Glaze them with a little milk and cook on the centre shelf of the oven for 10 minutes. Leave to cool on a wire rack.

Parmesan Herb Bread can be made a few days ahead of serving.

HERB SCONES

MAKES ABOUT 8

225 g/8 oz self-raising flour
½ teaspoon salt
2 teaspoons icing sugar (optional)
2 teaspoons mixed herbs
few sprigs fresh parsley, chopped
25 g/1 oz butter
120-175 ml/4-6 fl oz milk (or ½ milk, ½
water)

Sift the flour, salt and sugar (if used) into a bowl. Add the mixed herbs, parsley and butter and rub together with your fingertips until it resembles fresh breadcrumbs.

Mixing with a fork, add just enough milk (or milk and water) to make a soft dough. Turn out on to a lightly floured board and knead until the dough is smooth. Roll out to 2 cm/¾ inch thick and cut in 5 cm/2 inch rounds with a scone cutter.

Heat the oven to moderately hot, 200°C/400°F, Gas Mark 6. Place on a greased oven tray and bake in the oven for 12-15 minutes. Remove from the oven and cool.

FLAVOURED BREAD

Make your choice of herbs for bread or rolls to suit the dish they will accompany: dill, chervil or parsley for fish dishes; rosemary or tarragon with chicken; sage with pork; basil with pasta dishes or ratatouille; chives with cheeses. Just a pinch of the freshly chopped herb adds a lot of flavour – serve a herb butter to match.

SANDWICHES & PICNIC LOAVES

BAKED PICNIC LOAF

SERVES 8-10

1 large fresh white loaf
3 tablespoons melted butter
175 g/6 oz pistachio nuts, peeled
1 egg, beaten with a pinch of salt

FILLING:
40 g/1½ oz unsalted butter
1 medium onion, peeled and chopped
2 spring onions, chopped
1 clove garlic, peeled and crushed
100 g/4 oz pork, minced
100 g/4 oz veal, minced
450 g/1 lb packet frozen leaf spinach,
  thawed, drained and squeezed dry
150 g/5 oz leg ham, chopped finely
2 tablespoons freshly chopped parsley
1 egg, beaten lightly
½ teaspoon dried sage
pinch of ground nutmeg
salt and freshly ground black pepper
½ tablespoon freshly chopped rosemary
  leaves
2 teaspoons cognac
1 tablespoon single cream

Cut the top third off the bread and hollow out both top and bottom sections to leave shells 2 cm/¾ inch thick. Reserve the crumbs for the filling. Stand the shells in a warm, dry place for 1-2 hours, or until they are dry. Heat the oven to moderate 180°C/350°F, Gas Mark 4. Spread the crumbs on a baking sheet and bake in the oven for 5-10 minutes. When cool, process into fine breadcrumbs.
TO MAKE THE FILLING: melt the butter in a small saucepan over a moderate heat. Sauté the onions, spring onions and garlic until soft. Transfer to a large bowl. Cook the minced meat in the same pan, stirring until lightly browned. Add it to the onions in the bowl. Add all the remaining ingredients for the filling and combine well.
TO ASSEMBLE AND COOK THE LOAF: brush the insides of the crust shells with the melted butter. Spoon half the filling into the bottom shell. Sprinkle a layer of pistachio nuts down the centre. Pile the remainder of the filling on top and shape it to fit the top of the loaf. Brush the cut edges and the inside of the top shell with beaten egg and fit the top of the loaf back firmly in place. Heat the oven to moderately hot, 190°C/375°F, Gas Mark 5. Wrap the loaf tightly in foil and bake for 1 hour. Make the loaf on the day of the picnic – do not refrigerate.

Baked Picnic Loaf is delicious as well as being easy to transport.

PROVENÇAL BAGUETTES

MAKES 10 SLICES

350 g/12 oz sausagemeat
3 tablespoons olive oil
2×25 cm/10 inch long French bread
  sticks
1×425 g/13½ oz can peeled Italian
  tomatoes, drained and chopped
  coarsely
6 spring onions, sliced thinly
100 g/4 oz black olives, pitted and
  chopped finely
100 g/4 oz green olives, pitted and
  chopped finely
2 tablespoons capers
2 tablespoons finely chopped fresh
  basil
½ teaspoon dried ground thyme
½ teaspoon crushed garlic
½ teaspoon coarsely ground black
  pepper
salt to taste

Break up the sausagemeat with a fork. Heat the olive oil in a frying pan over a moderate heat and fry the sausagemeat until well browned. Set aside. Cut the ends off the bread sticks and, using a long thin knife, hollow out each centre. Place the ends of the sticks and the bread from the centres in a food processor and process to make breadcrumbs. Mix the breadcrumbs with the tomatoes, onions, olives, capers, herbs, seasonings and undrained sausagemeat. Use this filling to stuff the hollowed-out bread sticks. Wrap them tightly in foil and chill for 8 hours. Cut in 5 cm/2 inch individual slices to serve.

CUCUMBER AND WATERCRESS SANDWICHES

Do not make cucumber sandwiches more than 3 hours before serving.

MAKES 24

*1 loaf brown or white bread, sliced thinly
  into 24 slices
100 g/4 oz butter, softened
120 ml/4 fl oz Classic Mayonnaise (see
  page 41)
2 young cucumbers, peeled and sliced
  thinly
1 bunch watercress
salt and freshly ground black pepper*

Butter the bread. Spread 12 slices with the mayonnaise. On the remainder, place slices of cucumber and sprigs of watercress. Season well. Top each open sandwich with a mayonnaise-spread slice. Cut off the crusts. Keep in a cool place until required.

HERB SANDWICHES

MAKES 12

*1 large wholewheat or pumpernickel loaf,
  sliced
225 g/8 oz cream cheese
3 tablespoons freshly chopped mixed herbs
  (lovage, basil, thyme, tarragon)
2 stalks celery, chopped finely
3-4 pickled cucumbers, chopped finely
  (optional)*

Spread the bread with cheese and scatter half the slices with herbs, chopped celery (choose very white stalks for the sweetest flavour) and cucumbers, if used. Top with the remaining bread and wrap in clingfilm until needed, Cut in half to serve.

EGG AND STUFFED OLIVE SANDWICHES

MAKES 24

*1 loaf white or brown sliced bread
100 g/4 oz butter, softened
8 hard-boiled eggs, mashed
100 g/4 oz stuffed olives, sliced
1 tablespoon Classic Mayonnaise (see
  page 41)
salt
freshly ground black pepper*

Butter the bread. Combine the eggs, olives, mayonnaise and salt and pepper. Spread this mixture on half the bread and top with the remaining buttered slices. Cut off the crusts. Wrap the sandwiches in clingfilm and keep them cool until required. Cut in half or quarters to serve.

PRAWN AND CELERY SANDWICHES

MAKES 24

*2 loaves white bread, sliced thinly
225 g/8 oz butter, softened
3 tablespoons Classic Mayonnaise (see
  page 41)
2 kg/4 lb prawns, peeled, cleaned and
  chopped
2-3 stalks celery, chopped finely
salt
freshly ground black pepper.*

Butter the bread. Spread half the slices with mayonnaise; on the remainder place the chopped prawns and celery, and season to taste. Press the sandwiches together firmly. Cut away the crusts. Wrap the sandwiches in clingfilm and refrigerate until required. Cut in half to serve. Carry to the picnic in an insulated container.

SMOKED SALMON SANDWICHES

MAKES ABOUT 20

*1 sandwich loaf wholewheat bread, sliced
  thinly
100 g/4 oz butter, softened
1 tablespoon freshly chopped dill
  (optional)
approximately 500 g/1¼ lb smoked
  salmon, sliced very thinly
freshly ground white pepper*

Butter the bread. If you are using dill, strew a little over half of the slices. On top of the dill place a single layer of smoked salmon. Grind a very little white pepper over the salmon. Top with a slice of buttered bread and press firmly together. Trim off the crusts and wrap the sandwiches in clingfilm. Keep in a cool place until required. Cut in quarters to serve.

SANDWICH FILLINGS

Sandwiches are traditional picnic food. Be sure to use top-quality butter and the best bread, and spread the butter right to the edge of each slice. Apart from the recipes given here, you might like to try a selection of the following fillings:

● smoked beef with pickled cucumbers
● tuna fish, mayonnaise and tomatoes
● young spinach leaves with chopped bacon and sliced tomato
● cream cheese, ham and pineapple
● Italian salami, chopped egg and olives
● pork pâté with chopped prunes

PÂTÉ EN CROÛTE

(Pâté in a Pastry Case)

SERVES 8-10

PASTRY:
350 g/12 oz plain flour
½ teaspoon salt
225 g/8 oz butter, cut in small pieces
2 egg yolks beaten with 4 tablespoons cold
    water
1 egg, beaten with 1 tablespoon water to
    glaze

MARINADE:
4 tablespoons brandy
sprigs of fresh thyme and sage
freshly ground black pepper

FILLING:
100 g/4 oz ham, cut in thin strips
200 g/7 oz thinly cut lean veal, cut in
    strips
225 g/8 oz trimmed lean veal, cut in
    large dice
100 g/4 oz lamb's liver, cut in large dice
225 g/8 oz belly pork, cut in large dice
150 g/5 oz white breadcrumbs
1 clove garlic, peeled and crushed
1 teaspoon salt
freshly ground black pepper
½ teaspoon dried thyme
1 tablespoon chopped parsley
2 eggs, beaten
25 g/1 oz butter
100 g/4 oz mushrooms, chopped finely

TO MAKE THE PASTRY: sift the flour and salt into a food processor. Add the butter and process with an on-off action until mixture resembles coarse breadcrumbs. Pour in the egg yolks and process until the dough forms a ball. Wrap the dough in clingfilm, form it into an even flat cake and let it rest in the refrigerator for 1 hour.

TO MAKE THE FILLING: place the ham and veal strips in a shallow dish. Add the marinade ingredients, stir once or twice and leave to stand for at least 1 hour. Process the diced veal, liver and belly pork in a food processor with an on-off action until it resembles coarse mince. Do not cut the meat too finely. Place the mince in a bowl with the breadcrumbs, garlic, salt, pepper, dried thyme, parsley and beaten eggs. Heat the butter in a frying pan over a moderate heat and fry the mushrooms for 4-5 minutes. Add them to the other ingredients in the bowl and mix well together.

TO LINE THE TIN: roll out the pastry on a floured board. Butter a 28 cm/11 inch oblong cake tin and line it with pastry, leaving enough to cover the top and to make a few leaves and flowers for decoration.

It may be difficult to lift the rich pastry in one piece, so place manageable pieces in the tin and press them well down with your fingers to ensure that the tin is evenly lined. Wet the tin around the top with a little water to make the pastry stick when it is cooking.

TO FILL THE TIN: place one-third of the filling in a layer. Arrange half the marinated strips of meat lengthways on top. Add another layer of filling, more strips and the last of the filling. Press well to even the top. Roll out the rest of the pastry, drape it over the top and trim the edges. Press the edges together well with the tines of a fork.

Insert a large skewer into the centre of the pâté en croûte. Cut a small strip of pastry and wet the end. Wrap it around the skewer to form a flower. Remove the skewer and mould a tiny funnel of aluminium foil to place in the centre of the flower to enable steam to escape during baking. Cut 4 leaves from pastry trimmings and stick them around the flower with a little water.

TO COOK THE PÂTÉ EN CROÛTE: heat the oven to moderate, 180°C/350°F, Gas Mark 4. Bake the pâté in the centre of the oven for 1 hour 10 minutes. Remove from the oven and paint the top with egg wash, to glaze the pastry as it cooks. Return the pâté to the oven and cook for a further 20 minutes.

Remove the pâté from the oven and leave it in the tin to cool for 30 minutes before turning it out on to wire rack. Slide it out on its side, and carefully turn it the right way up so the top does not break.

PIZZETTE

MAKES 30

PASTRY:
3 tablespoons fresh yeast
6 tablespoons tepid water
225 g /8 oz plain flour
pinch of salt
1 tablespoon olive oil

TOPPING:
4 large tomatoes, skinned and chopped
225 g/8 oz mozzarella cheese, grated
1 tablespoon fresh oregano leaves
8 uncooked prawns, peeled
1 small sweet red pepper, seeded and
    sliced thinly
1 small sweet green pepper, seeded and
    sliced thinly
8 black olives, pitted
4 anchovies, drained
1-2 tablespoons olive oil
freshly ground black pepper
salt (if necessary)

TO MAKE THE DOUGH: place the yeast in a small bowl with the tepid water and stir to dissolve. Leave in a warm place to activate.

Make lots of little Pizzette – very tempting and sure to vanish fast.

Place the flour on a work surface and make a well in the centre. Add the salt, pour in the olive oil and yeast and combine with the fingertips to make a soft, firm elastic dough. Set aside, covered, in a warm place and leave for 1 hour until well risen. Work small pieces of dough into circles about 3.5 cm/1¼ inches in diameter.

TO MAKE THE TOPPING: press the tomatoes through a sieve or process in a blender to make a purée. Spread some purée on each of the pizzette. Sprinkle over the mozzarella, oregano and combinations of prawns, peppers, olives and anchovies. Sprinkle with olive oil and pepper and salt.

Heat the oven to hot, 200°-220°C/400°-425°F, Gas mark 6-7. Place the pizzette on an oiled baking sheet and bake for 5-8 minutes.

LEEK QUICHE

SERVES 6

PASTRY:
150 g/5 oz plain flour
100 g/4 oz butter straight from the refrigerator
pinch of salt
1½ tablespoons iced water

FILLING:
50 g/2 oz butter
1 tablespoon vegetable oil
750 g/1½ lb finely sliced leeks
1 tablespoon plain flour
2 eggs plus 1 egg yolk, beaten together
175 ml/6 fl oz single cream
salt
freshly ground black pepper
pinch of nutmeg
50 g/2 oz gruyère cheese, grated

TO MAKE THE PASTRY: put the flour, butter and salt in a food processor and run the machine with an on/off action until the mixture resembles breadcrumbs. Add the water all at once with the motor running and process until the dough forms a mass. If making pastry by hand, sift the flour and salt into a bowl. Rub in the butter and add the water to the flour gradually, mixing with a knife to form a dough. Form the dough into a ball and flatten it slightly. Wrap in cling-film and refrigerate for 1 hour.

TO COOK THE PASTRY CASE: heat the oven to moderately hot, 200°C/400°F, Gas Mark 6. Roll out the pastry on a floured board and use to line a 20 cm/8 inch quiche tin. Prick the bottom of the pastry with a fork to keep it from rising. Put a piece of greaseproof paper in the pastry case. Fill with beans or rice and cook in the middle of the oven for 8-10 minutes until the pastry is starting to colour and just beginning to shrink from

the sides of the tin. Remove the paper and beans or rice and prick the base with a fork. Return to the oven for 2-3 more minutes.

TO MAKE THE FILLING: heat the butter and oil in a frying pan over a moderate heat. Cook the leeks until they are just beginning to take colour. Sprinkle with flour, mix well and cook for 2-3 minutes. Remove from the heat and leave to cool slightly.

In a bowl beat together the eggs, cream, seasoning and nutmeg. Fold in the leeks and half of the cheese. Check the seasoning.

TO COOK THE QUICHE: reduce the oven temperature to 190°C/375°F, Gas Mark 5. Pour the filling into the pastry shell. Sprinkle over the remaining cheese. Bake on a shelf above the centre of the oven for 25-30 minutes, or until the filling is brown and set.

QUICHE FILLINGS

Versatile quiches form the basis of a tremendous range of dishes suitable for buffets as well as picnics and parties. Try some of these fillings:
- very finely sliced waxy potatoes with chives and cream
- smoked salmon with sliced courgettes
- asparagus and diced ham
- smoked haddock or cod with a scattering of chopped tomato
- spinach, flavoured with cumin and coriander and garnished with orange slices
- crabmeat with sweetcorn
- aubergine, tomato and onion
- mushrooms, sorrel and herbs
- cheese, bacon and halved prunes
- chopped anchovies, chillies and tomato

CRAB CREAM

SERVES 8

40 g/1½ oz butter
15 g/½ oz plain flour
250 ml/8 fl oz boiling chicken stock
1 tablespoon gelatine
450 g/1 lb crab meat
250 ml/8 fl oz Classic Mayonnaise (page 41)
300 ml/½ pint double cream, whipped
Tabasco sauce
salt and freshly ground pepper

GARNISH:
1 or 2 cucumbers, sliced thinly
225 g/8 oz cherry tomatoes
parsley sprigs
250 ml/8 fl oz Basic Vinaigrette (page 40)

Melt the butter in a saucepan set over a moderate heat. Stir in the flour and cook for 1 minute, still stirring. Pour 2 tablespoons of chicken stock into a small bowl. Add the remainder to the saucepan, stirring well, and whisk until the sauce is smooth and comes to the boil. Pour into a bowl and leave to cool.

To the small bowl of chicken stock add the gelatine, stirring well to dissolve it completely. Mix into the sauce. Fold in the crab meat, mayonnaise, cream and a dash or two of Tabasco sauce. Add salt and pepper to taste.

Oil a ring mould and pour in the crab meat. Cover and refrigerate for 4-6 hours. Take to the picnic in the ring mould.

TO SERVE: turn out the cream on to a serving platter. Arrange the cucumber slices, cherry tomatoes and parsley around the edge of the mould and fill the centre with cherry tomatoes. Drizzle vinaigrette over the garnish. Spoon the cream on to individual plates to serve (it is too soft to cut in slices).

SALMON AND PRAWN MOUSSE

SERVES 10-12

1 × 440 g/14 oz can red salmon
2 tablespoons gelatine
3 tablespoons warm water
450 g/1 lb cooked prawns, peeled and chopped
1½ tablespoons freshly chopped chives
1 tablespoon freshly chopped Italian parsley
6 spring onions, chopped (white part and some of the green)
2 tablespoons lemon juice
250 ml/8 fl oz Classic Mayonnaise (see page 41)
250 ml/8 fl oz double cream
dash of Tabasco sauce
salt and freshly ground black pepper
1 tablespoon oil

GARNISH:
continental cucumbers or fresh gherkins, cut lengthways

Remove skin and bones from the salmon. Using 2 forks, break up all the flesh into a bowl. Dissolve the gelatine in the warm water. Add prawns, chives, parsley, spring onions, lemon juice and gelatine to the salmon. Mix all the ingredients well. Add the mayonnaise and cream and mix well again. Add 2-3 drops of Tabasco and season.

Lightly oil a 25 cm × 8 cm/10 inch × 3½ inch oblong cake tin and spoon in the mixture. Cover with clingfilm and refrigerate overnight. Transport to the picnic in an insulated container.

TO SERVE: cut in slices and serve garnished with continental cucumbers or gherkins.

(Left) **Light-as-a-feather Crab Cream makes an eye-catching centrepiece.**

TROUT AND SMOKED SALMON RILLETTES

SERVES 8

*225 g/8 oz fresh trout, skinned and boned
  before weighing*
¼ teaspoon salt
175 g/6 oz unsalted butter
4 shallots, cut very finely
1 tablespoon white wine
*100 g/4 oz smoked salmon, roughly cut in
  small pieces*
2 tablespoons vegetable oil
1 egg yolk
1 tablespoon lemon juice
freshly ground white pepper
good pinch ground nutmeg
1 quantity Cucumber Vinaigrette (page 44)

Sprinkle the trout fillets with salt and leave them to stand for 30 minutes. Heat 25 g/1 oz butter in a frying pan and slowly cook the shallots until they are soft. Add the wine and trout, cover and cook for 3-4 minutes until the fish is cooked. Set aside.

Process the remaining butter in a food processor, using the clingfilm blade (or beat it vigorously in a bowl with a wooden spoon until pale and creamy). Flake the trout and add it in with all its cooking juices and the shallots. Drop in the smoked salmon pieces, oil, egg yolk, lemon juice, pepper and nutmeg. Process as little as possible, just enough to amalgamate the ingredients – the texture should be coarse. Alternatively beat well by hand until the ingredients are evenly combined. Pack the mixture into a bowl or china terrine. Smooth the surface with a palette knife. Cover the terrine and stand it in the refrigerator for 3 hours.

Remove the terrine from the refrigerator 1 hour before serving. Serve with a little Cucumber Vinaigrette (see page 44).

A pâté or terrine served with simple seasonal foods has a heart-of-the-country air and is no trouble to prepare.

ITALIAN VEGETABLE TERRINE WITH BASIL VINAIGRETTE

SERVES 8

750 ml/1¼ pints fresh tomato purée
10 basil leaves
1 teaspoon sugar
15 g/½ oz gelatine
dash of Tabasco sauce
salt
freshly ground white pepper
1 sweet green pepper
1 sweet red pepper
1 medium aubergine
oil for frying
4 green courgettes
4 yellow courgettes

BASIL VINAIGRETTE:
1 teaspoon Dijon mustard
juice of 1 lemon
½ bunch fresh basil
120 ml/4 fl oz peanut oil
120 ml/4 fl oz olive oil
salt
freshly ground black pepper

TO MAKE THE TERRINE: place the tomato purée in a blender with the basil leaves and sugar and work briefly. Transfer the purée to a medium saucepan over a moderate heat and bring it to simmering point. Remove the pan from the heat and leave it to cool. Melt the gelatine in a little hot water and stir it into the cooled purée. Add Tabasco and seasoning to taste.

TO PREPARE THE VEGETABLES: heat the oven to moderately hot, 200°C/400°F, Gas Mark 6. Bake the peppers for 20 minutes. Remove them from the oven and leave to cool. Peel off the skin, remove the seeds and stalks and chop the flesh into small cubes.

Cut the aubergine into 2 cm/¾ inch cubes. Heat the oil in a frying pan over a moderate heat and fry the aubergine until softened and slightly browned. Remove from the pan with a slotted spoon and drain on paper towels.

Halve the courgettes lengthways and blanch them for a few minutes in a saucepan of boiling salted water. Drain them well and refresh under cold water. Drain again and pat dry.

TO ASSEMBLE THE TERRINE: pour a thin layer of tomato purée in the bottom of an oiled 1.5 litre/2½ pint terrine dish and place it in the refrigerator. When this first layer has set, arrange the vegetables in the terrine in layers, alternating with a few spoonfuls of purée. When all the vegetables have been used, pour over the remaining purée, cover and place it in the refrigerator to set.

TO MAKE THE BASIL VINAIGRETTE: combine the mustard and lemon juice briefly in a blender. With the motor still running, add the fresh basil and pour in the oils. Add salt and pepper to taste.

TO SERVE: turn the terrine out on to a flat plate and slice it carefully into 8 pieces. Serve the basil vinaigrette separately.

Delicate layered Italian Vegetable Terrine with Basil Vinaigrette.

WHOLE DUCK TERRINE

SERVES 12

1×3 kg/6½ lb duck, skinned and boned
200 g/7 oz pork shoulder, cubed
200 g/7 oz veal shoulder, cubed
1 clove garlic, peeled and crushed
25 g/1 oz butter
100 g/4 oz onion, peeled and chopped
200 g/7 oz pigs' liver, cubed
200 g/7 oz belly pork, cubed
1 duck liver
4 tablespoons madeira
2 eggs, beaten
salt
½ tablespoon ground allspice
pepper
½ teaspoon dried thyme
a good pinch of ground cloves
275 g/10 oz cooked ham, cut in strips
2 tablespoons chopped shallots
pinch of thyme
4 tablespoons brandy
1 bay leaf
350 g/12 oz back fat, sliced thinly

Remove the duck breast in 2 pieces and set them aside. Chop the rest of the duck meat in small cubes. Mix it with the cubed pork and veal and crushed garlic in a large bowl. Melt the butter in a frying pan and fry the onion until soft, Add the pigs' liver, belly pork and duck liver and sauté for 2-3 minutes. Add this mixture to the meats in the bowl. Deglaze the pan with madeira and pour it into the bowl.

Blend the mixture in a food processor without making it too smooth. Transfer to a large bowl. Add the eggs, 1 tablespoon salt, allspice, ½ teaspoon pepper, thyme and cloves and combine well. Chill, covered, in the refrigerator for 24 hours.

Cut the 2 pieces of duck breast in strips. Place them in a bowl with the ham strips, shallots, thyme, brandy, bay leaf, ½ teaspoon salt and ¼ teaspoon pepper. Cover and refrigerate for 24 hours.

TO ASSEMBLE AND COOK THE TERRINE: heat the oven to moderate, 160°C/325°F, Gas Mark 3. Lift the strips of ham and duck breast out of the bowl and wipe dry. Line a 2-litre/3½ pint terrine with the slices of back fat. Pack in half the processed duck mixture, then alternate strips of ham and duck breast. Top with the remaining mixture. Cover with foil and bake in a bain-marie or tin of water in the oven for 1¾ hours. Remove the terrine from the water and leave to stand until cold. Place the terrine in the refrigerator overnight.

TO SERVE: turn out, cut in slices and serve with Spiced Orange Slices (see below).

SPICED ORANGE SLICES

SERVES 12

9 large oranges
1.5 kg/3 lb sugar
1½ cinnamon sticks
1½ heaped teaspoons cloves
450 ml/18 fl oz vinegar

Cut the unpeeled oranges in 5 cm/2 inch slices. Place in a large saucepan. Cover with water and simmer for about 1 hour or until tender. Drain.

In another saucepan, cook the sugar with the spices and vinegar to make a syrup. Place half the oranges in the pan and cook, covered, for 30 minutes. Remove them from the syrup and cook the rest of the oranges in the same way. Place the orange slices in a bowl, pour over the syrup and leave to stand for 24 hours.

Drain the orange slices and cook the syrup until it is thick. Add the orange slices and bring the syrup back to the boil. Transfer to hot clean jars and seal.

CHICKEN LIVER AND CHAMPAGNE PÂTÉ

SERVES 8

450 g/1 lb chicken livers, trimmed
25 g/1 oz plain flour
salt
freshly ground black pepper
40 g/1½ oz bacon fat
2 cloves garlic, peeled and chopped finely
100 g/4 oz mushrooms, sliced
about 120 ml/4 fl oz champagne

Dredge the cleaned chicken livers in flour seasoned with salt and pepper. Melt the bacon fat in a frying pan set over a moderate heat. Fry the garlic for 2 minutes. Increase the heat, add the livers and cook them for 3 minutes, turning several times. Add the mushrooms and cook for 1 minute longer. Adjust the seasoning.

Turn the mixture into the bowl of a blender or food processor. Add the champagne slowly, while the motor is running, until the mixture is smooth. Place in an earthenware dish and chill well in the refrigerator. Serve with crusty bread.

CHARCUTERIE TERMS

In modern cookery there is little difference between a pâté and a terrine, but originally there was a distinction – *pâté* referred to its pastry shell, while a *terrine* was the straight-sided terracotta dish in which a mixture of chopped meats (fat and lean) and flavourings was cooked.

PEARL BEACH PÂTÉ

SERVES 10

425 g/15 oz young lamb's liver pieces,
   skinned and trimmed
225 g/8 oz rindless bacon
5 fillets canned anchovies
1 clove garlic, peeled and crushed
freshly ground black pepper

BÉCHAMEL SAUCE:
250 ml/8 fl oz milk
1 onion, peeled and chopped
pinch of mace
1 bay leaf
4 peppercorns
40 g/1½ oz butter
40 g/1½ oz plain flour
350 g/12 oz thinly cut rindless bacon to
   line terrine or tin

GARNISH:
watercress

Mince the lamb's liver, bacon and anchovies very finely in a food processor with the garlic and pepper. Transfer to a mixing bowl. TO MAKE THE BÉCHAMEL SAUCE: put the milk, onion, mace, bay leaf and peppercorns in a saucepan over a moderate heat and bring slowly to the boil. In another saucepan melt the butter, add the flour and cook for 1 minute. Strain on the boiling liquid and beat with a whisk until the sauce is thick and smooth, and returns to the boil. Taste for salt and pepper. Add the sauce to the liver mixture and combine well.

Heat the oven to moderate, 160°C/325°F, Gas Mark 3. Line a terrine or tin with bacon and pour in the mixture. Bake in a bain-marie or baking dish in boiling water in the oven for 1 hour. Refrigerate for 24 hours.

To serve, turn out onto a flat platter and garnish with watercress.

PORK RILLETTES

SERVES 8-10

1 kg/2 lb belly pork, cut in large
   pieces
4 or 5 pork ribs, cut in 4 cm/1½
   inch lengths
1 pig's trotter, chopped in half
   lengthways
450 g/1 lb neck pork, cut in pieces
225 g/8 oz back fat, cut in pieces
1 clove garlic, peeled and crushed
1 sprig thyme
2 juniper berries
1 bay leaf
½ stick cinnamon
salt
freshly ground black pepper
pinch of ground nutmeg
120 ml/4 fl oz water
250 ml/8 fl oz white wine

Heat the oven to cool, 150°C/300°F, Gas Mark 2. Place all the ingredients in large, heavy casserole. Cover first with foil, then a lid and cook on the centre shelf of the oven for 5 hours. The meat will fall to pieces easily. Strain, reserving the liquid.

Remove the meat from the bones and discard the bones. Remove the bay leaf, thyme, juniper berries and cinnamon. Allow the meat to cool a little and break it up with two forks until both the meat and fat are completely shredded. Add the reserved liquid (including the fat) and beat with a fork until the mixture is well amalgamated, thick and creamy.

With care, you can break up the meat in a food processor, using the plastic blade. Do not use a steel blade or the rillettes will be pulverised instead of having a thready and creamy consistency.

Taste for salt, pepper and nutmeg. Pack the rillette mixture into a large earthenware bowl, cover and refrigerate.

TO SERVE: remove the rillettes from the refrigerator and let them stand until they reach room temperature. They should be soft, with a spreadable consistency. Serve with French bread and chutney.

PÂTÉ DE LAPIN

(Rabbit Pâté)

SERVES 6-8

meat from 1 large rabbit, diced
salt
freshly ground black pepper
1 tablespoon freshly chopped parsley
1 sprig of fresh thyme, chopped
750 g/1½ lb shoulder of pork, diced
3 shallots, peeled and chopped finely
120 ml/4 fl oz cognac
120 ml/4 fl oz white wine
350 g/12 oz bacon rashers
1 bay leaf

Place the rabbit flesh in a large bowl with salt and pepper, parsley, thyme, diced pork and shallots. Pour over the cognac and wine. Cover and stand in the refrigerator for 24 hours.

Line a terrine dish with bacon rashers. Pack in the meat and marinade, put a bay leaf on top and cover it with bacon. Heat the oven to moderate, 180°C/350°F, Gas Mark 4. Cover the terrine with a double layer of foil and cook in a bain-marie or baking dish in boiling water in the oven for 2 hours.

When the pâté is cooked, remove it from the oven and leave to stand with a weight on top until it is cold. Refrigerate for 24 hours before serving.

Variation on a theme. Clockwise from top: Pecan and Mushroom Salad (see page 47), *Pecan Terrine, and Skewered Chicken with Pecans* (see page 20).

PECAN TERRINE

SERVES 6

100 g/4 oz pork, minced
100 g/4 oz veal, minced
225 g/8 oz chicken thigh fillets, cut in small pieces
4 rashers rindless bacon, chopped
1 small onion, peeled and chopped finely
1 clove garlic, peeled and crushed
1 teaspoon freshly chopped tarragon
½ chicken stock cube, crumbled
salt
freshly ground black pepper
40 g/1½ oz toasted pecan nuts, chopped
50 g/2 oz mushrooms, chopped
½ teaspoon gelatine, optional

GARNISH:
tarragon or chervil leaves

Heat the oven to moderate, 180°/350°F, Gas Mark 4. Line an 18×9×5 cm/7×3½×2 inch loaf tin with foil, allowing the foil to extend 5 cm/2 inches above the tin all round. Combine the pork, veal, chicken and 2 rashers of chopped bacon in a bowl with the onion, garlic, tarragon and chicken stock cube. Season to taste. In a separate bowl, combine the pecan nuts, mushrooms and the remaining chopped bacon. Put one-third of the meat mixture in the prepared tin, pressing it well into the corners. Cover with half the pecan and mushroom mixture and continue layering in this way, finishing with the pork and veal mixture.

Put a strip of foil down the centre of the loaf and turn in the extended foil to completely cover the loaf. Cook in the oven for 50 minutes-1 hour, or until the juices are no longer pink and the meat is cooked. Remove the covering foil for the last 15-20 minutes. Allow to cool slightly. Pour or siphon out all the juices. If the juices did not reach the top of the loaf tin you will need to add a little water. Dissolve the gelatine in a little water and add it to the hot stock. Mix well to dissolve and pour into a container. Allow to cool and refrigerate overnight.

Meantime, re-cover the loaf with the foil and place on top another loaf tin, if available (otherwise use firm, foil-covered cardboard) and weigh down with weights adding up to about 1 kg/2 lb. This will help give the loaf a compact shape.

Next day, remove the fat from the chilled stock. Melt the stock over a gentle heat. Remove the loaf from the tin, discard the foil and return the loaf to the washed tin. Centre the loaf in the tin and pour in the stock. Chill until quite set then turn out on to a serving dish. (Dip the tin briefly in warm water to assist turning out.)
TO SERVE: garnish with tarragon or chervil. Serve cut in fairly thin slices.

VEGETARIAN PÂTÉS

Delicious pâtés can be made from a base of fresh ricotta cheese, or cooked and puréed beans or pulses flavoured with herbs and spices, onion, garlic, mushrooms, apple or cranberries. Avoid gelatine, an unacceptable animal product.

CHICKEN STUFFED WITH MANGO, WALNUTS AND SULTANAS

SERVES 6

*1 chicken (weighing 1.8 kg/
  3 lb 12 oz)
100 g/4 oz butter, melted*

STUFFING:
*1 mango, peeled and chopped
25 g/1 oz fresh breadcrumbs
15 g/½ oz butter
25 g/1 oz walnuts, chopped
25 g/1 oz sultanas
1 egg yolk, beaten
salt and freshly ground black pepper*

TO BONE THE CHICKEN: place the chicken breast side down on the work surface. With a sharp knife, slice down the backbone from neck end to tail. Cut off the tail and cut off the wing tips at the joints. Pushing the flesh with your fingers, remove the rib cage to the point where it meets the wing and leg joints. Cut through the joints and continue in the same manner until only the thin strip joining the two half breasts remains. Cut through the thin layer of flesh, being careful not to cut the skin. Remove the rib cage.

With the knife blade, scrape the flesh from the thigh bones and continue down to the end of the leg bone. Cut around the skin at the end of the bone to release it. Repeat with the wing bones. Spread the chicken meat on a large board, skin side down.

TO STUFF THE CHICKEN: mix all the ingredients for the stuffing together in a bowl. Form the mixture into a roll and place it down the centre of the chicken. Roll up and tie the chicken with fine string at 2 cm/¾ inch intervals. Tuck in the ends and tie the chicken lengthways to keep the roll secure.

TO COOK THE CHICKEN: heat the oven to moderately hot, 200°C/400°F, Gas Mark 6. Place the chicken in a small baking tin and pour over the melted butter. Cook on the centre shelf of the oven, basting from time to time, for 1 hour.

Remove from the oven and transfer to a shallow dish. Leave to cool completely then place in the refrigerator for 1-2 hours. To serve, cut in slices.

CHICKEN WITH PESTO MAYONNAISE

SERVES 8

*1 chicken (weighing 1.75 kg/4 lb)
salt and freshly ground black pepper*

STUFFING:
*175 g/6 oz fresh breadcrumbs
2 tablespoons freshly chopped parsley
1 teaspoon freshly chopped mixed herbs
1-2 tablespoons soured cream
4 thin slices prosciutto
2 sweet red peppers, roasted to remove the
  skins, seeded and cut in strips (see
  Pepper Salad with Capers, page 44)
10-12 thin slices spicy salami
3 or 4 hard-boiled eggs
75 g/3 oz butter*

TO SERVE:
Pesto Mayonnaise (see recipe below)

TO BONE THE CHICKEN: follow the instructions given for Chicken Stuffed with Mango, Walnuts and Sultanas (see left), but leave the wing bones intact. Lay the chickens on a flat board and sprinkle with salt and pepper. Push the boned legs back into the body and use a meat mallet to flatten and evenly distribute the chicken flesh.

TO STUFF THE CHICKEN: mix together in a bowl the breadcrumbs and fresh herbs, and moisten with the soured cream. Spread this mixture on the chicken in one layer. Top it with a layer of prosciutto, a layer of red pepper strips and finally a layer of salami. Trim the ends of the hard-boiled eggs so that they sit firmly together. Place them down the centre of the chicken.

Roll up the chicken, tucking in the top and bottom to form a parcel. Secure with poultry pins and tie at intervals with twine. Rub the butter over the surface.

TO COOK THE CHICKEN: heat the oven to moderate, 180°C/350°F, Gas Mark 4. Place the chicken on a rack in a baking tin and roast in the oven for 1 hour. Remove the chicken from the oven, leave to cool completely and place in the refrigerator overnight. Serve sliced, with Pesto Mayonnaise (see below).

PESTO MAYONNAISE

SERVES 8

*3 egg yolks
1 tablespoon Dijon mustard
1 tablespoon white wine vinegar
salt
pepper
300 ml/½ pint peanut oil*

PESTO SAUCE:
*6 tablespoons basil leaves, chopped finely
2 cloves garlic, peeled and chopped finely
salt
50 g/2 oz toasted pine nuts
50 g/2 oz freshly grated Parmesan cheese
4-5 tablespoons oil*

Place the egg yolks, mustard, wine vinegar, salt and pepper in a blender or food processor and process for a few seconds. With the motor still running, add the oil in a thin but steady stream to make a thick mayonnaise. Transfer to a bowl.

TO MAKE THE PESTO SAUCE: mix the basil, garlic, salt and pine nuts in a blender or food processor until the ingredients are combined. Mix in the cheese. With the motor still running, gradually add the oil until the sauce has the consistency of a purée.

TO MAKE THE PESTO MAYONNAISE: mix the mayonnaise with the pesto sauce in equal quantities, or to taste.

SMOKED DUCK WITH SOUR CHERRIES

SERVES 8

8 large breasts of duck, skinned and trimmed of excess fat

MARINADE:
600 ml/1 pint water
120 ml/4 fl oz Kirsch
50 g/2 oz salt
50 g/2 oz nitrite salt (from the chemist)
½ clove garlic, peeled and crushed
½ teaspoon peppercorns
½ teaspoon ground coriander
½ teaspoon fennel seeds
1 tablespoon honey
zest of 1 lemon
1 bay leaf

SOUR CHERRIES:
300 ml/½ pint white wine vinegar
100 g/4 oz clear honey
juice of 2 oranges
juice of 1 lemon
2 bay leaves
5 white peppercorns
5 black peppercorns
1 clove
sugar to taste
1 kg/2 lb cherries, washed and stoned

GARNISH:
celery strips
green herb leaves

Smoked Duck with Sour Cherries makes a subtle combination of flavours.

TO SMOKE THE DUCK: place the breasts in a single layer in a glass or ceramic dish. Combine all the marinade ingredients and pour the marinade over the duck. Leave in the refrigerator for 8 days to marinate. Remove the duck breasts from the liquid, pat them dry and cold smoke (below 30°C/86°F) for 1 hour a day for 3 consecutive days. Rest the duck in the refrigerator for 1 day.

TO PREPARE THE CHERRIES: place all the ingredients except cherries in a large saucepan set over a moderate heat. Bring to the boil, stirring to dissolve the sugar. Add the cherries. When the syrup comes back to the boil, drain the cherries carefully and leave them to cool in a covered container. Place in the refrigerator until serving time.

TO SERVE THE DUCK: line a serving platter with fine strips of celery. Slice the duck breasts thinly and arrange them on the top. Surround with the cherries and garnish with sprigs of green herb leaves.

TURKEY BREAST ROLL WITH ITALIAN SAUSAGE STUFFING

MAKES 16-18 SLICES

1 half turkey breast
25 g/1 oz butter, softened
salt
freshly ground black pepper
3 tablespoons chopped fresh herbs
*   (such as oregano, parsley, chives,*
*   sage or thyme)*
4 Italian-style fresh meat sausages
8 bacon rashers, rinds removed

Remove the skin from the turkey breast carefully and reserve. Slice the turkey breast lengthways with a sharp knife from one side almost to the other. Open out into one thick steak of turkey meat. Spread soft butter over the surface of the meat. Sprinkle it with salt, pepper and with the chopped fresh herbs.

Remove the sausage skins and form the meat into one large sausage. Place it across the turkey meat. Shape the turkey into a roll, using large and small skewers and poultry pins to hold it in place. Carefully spread the reserved skin over the turkey roll and secure it with pins. Wrap the bacon rashers around the turkey roll.

Heat the oven to moderately hot, 200°C/400°F, Gas Mark 6.

Wrap the roll in a double sheet of foil, securing it firmly so the juices do not run out. Place in a roasting tin and cook on the centre shelf of the oven for 55 minutes. Remove from the oven and allow to cool in the foil. Cut in slices to serve.

HERBED QUAIL

SERVES 12

12 quail, cleaned and dried
2 tablespoons freshly chopped mixed
*   herbs, such as oregano, thyme,*
*   marjoram*
salt
freshly ground black pepper
225 g/8 oz butter, melted

Heat the oven to hot, 220°C/425°F, Gas Mark 7. Place the birds in a large roasting tin, breast side up. Sprinkle with the herbs, salt and pepper. Pour on the melted butter. Bake on the centre shelf of the oven for 30 minutes. Baste twice during cooking.

When the birds are cooked, remove from the oven, cover loosely with foil and allow to cool.

If possible cook the quail about 30 minutes before leaving for the picnic. Do not refrigerate. The flavour will be better and the meat more moist.

CORIANDER CRUMBED CUTLETS

SERVES 6

12 lamb cutlets
2 tablespoons lemon juice
2 cloves garlic, peeled and crushed
250 ml/8 fl oz plain yoghurt
1 small chilli, minced, with seeds
50 g/2 oz fresh coriander, leaves and
*   roots, chopped*
100 g/4 oz breadcrumbs
salt
cayenne

GARNISH:
chopped coriander leaves
grated lemon rind

In a shallow baking dish, large enough to hold all the cutlets, combine the lemon juice, garlic, yoghurt, chilli and coriander. Place the cutlets in the dish, turning them to coat with the yoghurt mixture. Leave them to marinate for 6 hours.

Mix the breadcrumbs in a bowl with salt and cayenne. Remove the cutlets from the marinade, and without drying them turn them in the breadcrumbs until they are well coated. Refrigerate overnight.

Heat the oven to moderately hot, 200°C/400°F, Gas Mark 6. Place the cutlets on a greased baking tray and cook in the oven for 10 minutes each side until golden brown. Remove from the oven and leave to cool. Just before serving, sprinkle with coriander and lemon rind.

VEAL WITH GREEN PEPPERCORNS

SERVES 6

2 kg/4 lb veal loins
salt
coarse-grained mustard
1×50 g/2 oz can green peppercorns
15 g/½ oz butter
1 tablespoon oil

Ask the butcher to bone the meat and trim off any sinew. Lay the loins flat, season them with salt and spread with mustard, then sprinkle liberally with peppercorns. Roll up the meat and tie it with fine string.

Heat the oven to moderately hot, 190°C/375°F, Gas Mark 5. Heat the butter and oil in a roasting tin on top of the stove and brown the meat evenly on all sides. Cook in the oven for 45 minutes or until the juices run clear when the meat is pierced with a skewer. Remove from the oven and leave to cool. Chill in the refrigerator until needed. Serve the veal cut in slices.

QUINCE-GLAZED PORK WITH CARAWAY SEEDS

If quinces are not available, substitute red-currants and redcurrant jelly.

SERVES 8

1 neck of pork (boneless spare rib joint)
1 tablespoon oil
20 g/¾ oz butter
1 tablespoon water
250 ml/8 fl oz (or more) quince jelly
1 tablespoon brandy
caraway seeds

TO SERVE:
3 quinces
500 ml/18 fl oz red wine
juice of 1 lemon
1 lemon, sliced
225 g/8 oz sugar
½ teaspoon cinnamon

Heat the oven to moderate, 180°C/350°F, Gas Mark 4. Place the pork in a roasting tin with the oil, butter and water and bake in the oven for about 1½ hours.

Heat the quince jelly with the brandy in a saucepan set over a moderate heat. Use this to repeatedly glaze the pork in the last 30 minutes of cooking time.

When the pork is cooked, place it on a platter. Pour over the remaining quince jelly mixture and scatter with caraway seeds. Leave to cool completely.

Slice the quinces but leave the core and seeds intact. Place the wine, lemon juice, lemon slices, sugar and cinnamon in a saucepan over a moderate heat and bring to the boil. Add the quince slices and poach them gently until they are cooked and coloured. Transfer to a bowl and leave to cool. Remove the core and seeds. Serve with the glazed pork.

A substantial main course: Quince-glazed Neck of Pork with Caraway Seeds.

GLAZED GAMMON

A whole glazed gammon is the perfect party piece.

SERVES 25-30

1 whole gammon
1 pineapple, peeled and sliced very thinly
50 g/2 oz cloves
75 g/3 oz clear honey, melted over low heat
2 tablespoons granulated sugar

Soak the gammon overnight in a large container. Change the water. Set the pan over a moderate heat, bring to the boil, then reduce the heat and simmer for 30 minutes per kg/15 minutes per lb. Turn off the heat and leave in the cooking liquid to cool.

When the gammon is cool, remove the skin and cover the fatty top of the meat with the sliced pineapple, securing each slice with cloves. Heat the oven to moderately hot, 200°C/400°F, Gas Mark 6. Arrange the gammon carefully in a large baking dish. Pour over the heated honey, sprinkle with sugar and bake in the oven for 15 minutes.

Remove from the oven and leave to rest before serving, cut in thin slices.

JAMBON PERSILLÉ

(Ham with Parsley)

SERVES 10

½ a cooked ham, about 5 kg/11 lb, rind
 and thick fat removed
1 tablespoon gelatine
a handful of freshly chopped parsley

STOCK:
1.75 kg/4 lb veal neck and breast bones
2 pig's trotters
25 g/1 oz parsley
1 lemon, cut into quarters
2 carrots, peeled and chopped
2 celery stalks, chopped
2 onions, peeled and chopped
3 cloves garlic
sprig of thyme
freshly ground white pepper
1 bottle dry white wine
1 litre/1¾ pints water

Cut the ham from the bone in large pieces.
Trim off any dried smoked ham and discard
it. Cut the meat in 4-5 cm/1½-2 inch dice.
Place in a bowl, cover and refrigerate.

Put all the stock ingredients in a large saucepan, set over a moderate heat, cover and
bring to the boil. Reduce the heat and simmer for at least 3 hours until the meat falls
off the bones. Strain the stock into a bowl.
Pick the meat from the pig's trotters and
reserve it, but discard all the bones and
vegetables. Stand the bowl of stock in the
refrigerator overnight to set the fat. When it
is set, carefully remove the fat as completely
as possible.

Place the skimmed stock in a large saucepan and bring to a simmer. Add the meat
from the pig's trotters and ham. Simmer
gently, covered, for 30 minutes. Remove
from heat, add gelatine and stir until dissolved. Add 50 g/2 oz parsley and pepper to
taste (there will be enough salt in the ham).

Pour the mixture into a large white bowl.
Leave it to cool, cover the bowl and refrigerate overnight.

TO SERVE: sprinkle the ham with the remaining parsley and cut it in slices straight from
the bowl.

ROAST SIRLOIN WITH HERB BÉARNAISE SAUCE

SERVES 8-10

100 g/4 oz butter
piece of sirloin weighing about 4 kg/8¾ lb
sea salt
freshly ground pepper
1 teaspoon dried mixed herbs

HERB BÉARNAISE SAUCE:
6 egg yolks, beaten
1 tablespoon dried tarragon
6 tablespoons single cream
pinch of cayenne
¼ teaspoon salt
225 g/8 oz butter, cut in small pieces
1 tablespoon chopped chives
1 tablespoon chopped parsley
1 tablespoon lemon juice or white vinegar
salt
freshly ground white pepper

Heat the oven to moderately hot,
200°C/400°F, Gas Mark 6. Melt the butter in a
baking pan and place in the sirloin. Sprinkle
liberally with salt, pepper and herbs and
roast on the centre shelf of the oven for 1¼
hours, basting from time to time. When the
meat is cooked remove it from the oven and
leave it to cool in the pan.

TO MAKE THE HERB BÉARNAISE SAUCE: put the
beaten egg yolks, tarragon, cream, cayenne
and salt into the top of a double boiler over
simmering water. (Do not allow the water
to touch the pot of mixture or it will thicken
too quickly.) Whip with an egg whisk until
the mixture thickens a little. Remove from
the heat and whisk in the butter in small
pieces. Pour the thickened sauce into a bowl.
Mix in the chives, parsley and lemon juice
or vinegar. Add salt and pepper to taste.

TO SERVE: transfer the sirloin to a serving
platter and cut in slices. Serve the herb
béarnaise sauce separately in a bowl. It may
be served hot or cold.

FILLET OF BEEF WITH WALNUT STUFFING

SERVES 6

about 750 g/1½ lb fillet of beef, trimmed
 of fat and sinew
1 tablespoon French mustard
freshly ground black pepper
100 g/4 oz butter

WALNUT STUFFING:
25 g/1 oz butter
25 g/1 oz onions, peeled and chopped
 finely
25 g/1 oz walnuts, ground finely
1 egg, beaten
2 tablespoons finely chopped parsley
1 teaspoon finely grated orange rind
2 tablespoons port

TO MAKE THE STUFFING: melt the butter in a
small pan set over a moderate heat. Cook
the onions until soft. Remove the pan from
the heat and add the remaining ingredients,
stirring well to combine them smoothly.

TO STUFF THE FILLET: cut a slit lengthways in
the fillet. Rub the inside and outside thinly
with mustard and season with black pepper.
Fill the cavity neatly with the stuffing. Close
it up and tie with fine string so that it will

keep its shape and not open up.

TO COOK THE FILLET: heat the oven to hot, 220°/425°F, Gas Mark 7. Melt the butter in a roasting tin set on top of the cooker. Put the fillet in the tin and brown it all over, turning it carefully. Place the tin in the oven and cook for 8 minutes. Reduce the heat to moderate, 180°C/350°F, Gas Mark 4 and cook for a further 22 minutes at that heat. Remove the tin from the oven and leave the fillet to rest. It will go on cooking for some minutes. Transfer the meat to a serving dish and let it cool completely. Serve cold, cut in generous slices.

EGG AND BACON LOAF

SERVES 6

1 kg/2 lb lean steak, minced
1 teaspoon salt
freshly ground black pepper
50 g/2 oz fresh breadcrumbs
250 ml/8 fl oz milk
1 small onion, peeled and chopped finely
2 teaspoons chopped fresh or ½ teaspoon
  dried herbs, such as parsley, thyme,
  oregano and rosemary
3 hard-boiled eggs, shelled
2-3 rashers bacon, rinds removed

Heat the oven to moderate, 180°C/350°F, Gas Mark 4. In a mixing bowl, thoroughly combine all the ingredients except the eggs and bacon. Place a quarter of the mixture in a greased 21×15 cm/8½×6 inch loaf tin. Arrange the eggs down the middle and pack the remaining meat mixture around them. Smooth over the top. Cut the bacon rashers in half and arrange them on top. Bake the loaf in the oven for 1 hour or until it shrinks slightly from the sides of the tin.

TO SERVE: turn out on to a flat plate or board and cut into slices.

Clockwise from top: *Green Salad with Bean Sprouts* (see page 42), *Fillet of Beef with Walnut Stuffing, and Mange Tout and Artichoke Salad* (see page 42).

DESSERTS, CAKES & BISCUITS

PEACH AND MANGO SALAD WITH PASSIONFRUIT DRESSING

SERVES 6

6 large peaches, peeled
2 large mangoes, peeled

DRESSING:
juice of 2 oranges
pulp of 8 passionfruit or 1×75 g/3 oz can
pulp
2 tablespoons brandy
1 tablespoon castor sugar

Slice the peaches and mangoes in even diagonal pieces about 4 cm/1½ inches long. Place in individual containers.
TO MAKE THE DRESSING: combine the orange juice with the passionfruit pulp, brandy and castor sugar. Mix well until the sugar is dissolved. Place in a tightly sealed container and pour on to individual fruit salads at serving time.

FRESH FRUIT COMPOTE

SERVES 6

1 bottle sweet dessert wine
100 g/4 oz sugar
3 ripe yellow peaches, peeled and halved
3 ripe apricots, halved
4 figs, peeled and quartered
50 g/2 oz green grapes
50 g/2 oz black grapes
225 g/8 oz strawberries, hulled

Place the wine and sugar in a saucepan set over a moderate heat. Boil until reduced to half the original quantity. Place the fruit in a glass bowl and carefully pour over all the boiling syrup. Allow to cool, then chill in the refrigerator for 4 or 5 hours.

CARAMELISED ORANGES

SERVES 6

6 large oranges
100 g/4 oz sugar
250 ml/8 fl oz dry white wine
150 ml/¼ pint orange juice
120 ml/4 fl oz tawny port
4 tablespoons Grand Marnier

Peel the oranges, removing all the white pith. Cut each orange in half. Cut the peel in fine strips about the size of a matchstick and boil in water for 5 minutes.
   Bring the sugar, wine and orange juice to the boil in a small saucepan. Drain the orange peel and cook it in the syrup until the strips become transparent and caramelised. It is important to take care that the mixture does not burn.
TO SERVE: arrange the oranges in a serving dish and place little heaps of caramelised orange peel on top. Mix the port, Grand Marnier and left-over syrup together and pour over the oranges.

GREEN MELON WITH GINGER SUGAR

⅓ to ½ honeydew melon per person,
according to size of melon

GINGER SUGAR:
1 teaspoon ground ginger
6 tablespoons caster sugar

Remove the melon seeds. Chill the melon and slice it or peel it and dice the flesh. Place it on a handsome dessert plate. Mix the ginger and sugar together in a bowl and pass it for sprinkling on the melon pieces.

RED FRUIT SALAD

SERVES 6

6 red plums, stoned and quartered
350 g/12 oz strawberries, hulled
good-sized slice of watermelon, seeded
and diced
350 g/12 oz redcurrants
caster sugar
300 ml/½ pint single cream

Mix the prepared plums, strawberries and watermelon together on a large platter and dot tiny bunches of redcurrants on top.
   Serve the red fruit salad with a bowl of caster sugar and a jug of cream as soon as the fruit has been prepared.

GREEN CUISINE

A salad made up of fruits of one colour is a splendid way to end any meal – try a green variation on Red Fruit Salad (above), using white grapes, dessert gooseberries, greengages, apples, kiwifruit, pears and melons. Decorate with slivers of lime or sprigs of mint.

A crisp collection of plums, strawberries, watermelon and redcurrants make this Red Fruit Salad.

ITALIAN SWEET RICE AND GLACÉ FRUIT PIE

SERVES 8

PASTRY:
175 g/6 oz plain flour
75 g/3 oz caster sugar
1 egg
100 g/4 oz softened butter

FILLING:
500 ml/18 fl oz milk
250 ml/8 fl oz cold water
6-8 tablespoons sugar, to taste
175 g/6 oz short-grain rice
40 g/1½ oz butter
¼ teaspoon ground nutmeg
50 g/2 oz raisins
250 ml/8 fl oz hot water
1 egg, beaten
5 tablespoons chopped glacé fruits
3 tablespoons pine nuts
1 teaspoon vanilla essence
3 tablespoons brandy

TO DECORATE:
assorted glacé fruits, sliced
250 ml/8 fl oz whipping cream, whipped

Finish Italian Sweet Rice and Glacé Fruit Pie with a flourish of fruits.

TO MAKE THE PASTRY: place all the ingredients in a food processor and process until they form a smooth ball. Remove the dough from the machine and wrap it in clingfilm. Leave it to rest in the refrigerator for 1 hour.

TO MAKE THE FILLING: put the milk, water and sugar in a medium saucepan over a moderate heat, and bring to the boil, stirring well to dissolve the sugar. Add the rice, reduce the heat and continue to cook for about 15 minutes, stirring occasionally, until the liquid is absorbed and the rice is cooked. Stir in the butter and ground nutmeg and leave the rice to cool. Soak the raisins in hot water while the rice is cooking. Drain them thoroughly and add to the rice with the egg, chopped fruits, nuts, vanilla essence and brandy.

TO MAKE THE PIE: heat the oven to moderately hot, 200°C/400°F, Gas Mark 6. Roll out the pastry and use it to line a 23 cm/9 inch pie dish. Fill the pastry shell with the rice mixture. Place in the oven and bake for 40 minutes. Remove from the oven and leave to cool.

TO SERVE: decorate the finished pie with slices of glacé fruit and serve at the picnic with whipped cream.

FRIANDS

MAKES 12

100 g/4 oz ground almonds
100 g/4 oz caster sugar
4 egg whites
40 g/1½ oz plain flour, sifted
½ teaspoon vanilla essence
100 g/4 oz butter, melted and slightly
*   browned*
icing sugar, for dusting

Heat the oven to hot, 220°C/425°F, Gas Mark 7. In a bowl mix the ground almonds, sugar and egg whites together to form a paste. Add the flour and vanilla. Pour in the butter and beat well. Butter and flour 12 muffin tins and spoon in the mixture.

Cook the cakes on the centre shelf of the oven for 12 minutes. Remove from the oven and stand for 5 minutes before turning out to cool. Sift icing sugar over the cakes before serving.

POPPY SEED CAKE

MAKES 1 × 20 cm/8 inch RING CAKE

450 g/1 lb butter
350 g/12 oz sugar
2 tablespoons poppy seeds
1 teaspoon freshly grated nutmeg
pinch of ground mace
1 teaspoon grated lemon rind
6 eggs, separated
225 g/8 oz plain flour, sifted
a little milk, if necessary
icing sugar, for dusting

Heat the oven to moderate, 180°C/350°F, Gas Mark 4. Cream the butter in a large mixing bowl. Gradually add the sugar and beat until light and fluffy. Add the poppy seeds, nutmeg, mace and lemon rind. Beat in 6 egg yolks, then fold in the flour.

Beat the egg whites until they hold soft peaks and carefully fold them into the cake batter. If the batter seems very heavy before the egg whites are added, thin it with a little milk. Pour the batter into a buttered and floured 20 cm/8 inch ring tin.

Bake in the oven for 1½-2 hours. The cake is cooked when a skewer inserted into the centre comes out clean, and the cake is brown and firm to the touch. Turn out on a cake rack and allow to cool. When cold, dust with icing sugar.

RHUBARB CAKE

MAKES 1 × 23 cm/9 inch SQUARE CAKE

250 g/9 oz brown sugar
100 g/4 oz butter
2 eggs, beaten
250 ml/8 fl oz soured milk (2 tablespoons
*   vinegar in 250 ml/8 fl oz milk)*
1 teaspoon bicarbonate of soda
1 teaspoon salt
175 g/6 oz flour, sifted
1 teaspoon vanilla essence
225 g/8 oz rhubarb, sliced finely

TOPPING:
75 g/3 oz brown sugar
1 teaspoon ground cinnamon

Heat the oven to moderate, 180°C/350°F, Gas Mark 4. Cream the sugar with the butter until pale and fluffy. Add the eggs and beat well. Add the soured milk, bicarbonate of soda, salt, flour and vanilla. Mix well to make a smooth batter. Fold in the rhubarb. Pour the mixture into a greased and floured 23 cm/9 inch square cake tin.

Mix the brown sugar with the cinnamon and sprinkle on to the cake mixture.

Bake in the oven for 45 minutes. The cake is cooked when a skewer inserted in the centre comes out clean. Turn out on a cake rack and allow to cool.

APPLE PECAN NUT CAKE

MAKES 1 × 20 cm/8 inch SQUARE CAKE OR 10 SLICES

2 cooking apples, peeled, cored, and cut
*   in chunks*
225 g/8 oz sugar
175 g/6 oz plain flour
1 level teaspoon bicarbonate of soda
1 teaspoon cinnamon
1 teaspoon allspice
½ teaspoon salt
100 g/4 oz roughly chopped pecan nuts
1 egg
100 g/4 oz butter, melted
whipped cream, to serve (optional)

Heat the oven to moderate, 180°C/350°F, Gas Mark 4.

In a bowl combine the apples and sugar. Set aside. In a separate bowl, sift the flour, bicarbonate of soda, spices and salt. Mix in the chopped pecan nuts. Beat the egg into the cooled melted butter and add to the apples. Lightly mix in the flour-nut mixture and spoon into a greased 20 cm/8 inch square tin. Bake in the oven for 45-55 minutes.

Remove from the oven and leave to cool in the tin for 15 minutes. Turn out on to a wire rack to cool completely.

Serve the cake in slices with whipped cream if liked.

MELTING MOMENTS

MAKES 24

225 g/8 oz butter
50 g/2 oz icing sugar
175 g/6 oz plain flour, sifted
generous 50 g/2 oz cornflour
vanilla essence, to taste

Heat the oven to cool, 150°C/300°F, Gas Mark 2. Melt the butter in a small saucepan. Pour it into a large mixing bowl and leave to cool. Beat in the icing sugar. Add the flour, cornflour and vanilla. Butter 2 baking sheets and place teaspoonsful of the mixture on the sheets. Cook for 20 minutes in the oven. Remove from the oven and cool on a wire rack. Store in an airtight tin.

CRAIGMOOR SHORTBREAD

MAKES 12

225 g/8 oz plain flour
100 g/4 oz cornflour
100 g/4 oz caster sugar
225 g/8 oz unsalted butter
a few drops of almond or vanilla essence

Heat the oven to moderate, 160°C/325°F, Gas Mark 3. Put all the ingredients in a food processor and process with an on/off action until the mixture is smooth. Alternatively, sift together the flour and cornflour in a mixing bowl. Add the sugar and the almond or vanilla essence. Rub in the butter with the tips of your fingers until the dough is smooth. When the dough is made, turn on to a lightly floured board and knead lightly.

Roll out the dough to approximately 5 cm/2 inches thick on a greased baking sheet. Prick all over the top with a fork and mark the edges with the tines of a fork. Bake in the oven for 30-35 minutes until the shortbread is cooked but not brown. Let it cool for 10 minutes and then cut in pieces. Place on a wire rack to cool completely. Store in an airtight tin.

VIENNESE BISCUITS

MAKES 15

100 g/4 oz butter
1 tablespoon plus 1 teaspoon icing sugar
1 small egg, beaten
150 g/5 oz plain flour
50 g/2 oz dark chocolate, melted

Heat the oven to moderate, 180°C/350°F, Gas Mark 4. In a bowl, beat the butter and sugar until light and fluffy. Add the egg and flour and mix to a smooth paste.

Cover a baking tray with foil, oil it lightly and dust with flour. Using a piping bag and plain nozzle, pipe the mixture into fingers or horseshoe shapes. Cook in the oven until pale golden. Remove from the oven and leave to cool. When cold, remove from the foil and dip the ends into melted chocolate.

BUTTER BISCUITS

MAKES 36

100 g/4 oz butter
100 g/4 oz sugar
1 egg
½ teaspoon vanilla essence
½ teaspoon finely grated lemon rind
1 teaspoon finely grated orange rind
75 g/3 oz plain flour

Heat the oven to moderately hot, 190°C/375°F, Gas Mark 5. In a bowl beat the butter and sugar to a cream. Add the egg, vanilla and lemon and orange rind and beat again until the mixture is pale and fluffy. Mix the flour in well. Drop small teaspoons of the mixture 7.5 cm/3 inches apart on a buttered baking sheet. Bake on the centre shelf of the oven for 10 minutes or until the biscuits are golden around the edge. Remove from the oven and cool.

PECAN NUT BISCUITS

MAKES 30

100 g/4 oz butter
2 tablespoons caster sugar
1 teaspoon vanilla essence
100 g/4 oz plain flour, sifted before
  measuring
100 g/4 oz pecan nuts, processed finely
icing sugar, to glaze

Heat the oven to cool, 150°C/300°F, Gas Mark 2. Process together the butter, sugar and vanilla until pale and creamy. Add the flour and process until well blended. Stir in the nuts. Roll the mixture into small balls and place them on a buttered oven tray. Cook in the centre of the oven for 15 minutes. Remove from the oven and carefully roll the biscuits in icing sugar. Return to the oven and cook for 20 minutes more.

Remove from the oven and roll immediately in icing sugar once more. Cool on a wire rack and store in an airtight container.

NUT WAFER BISCUITS

MAKES 36

3 egg whites
100 g/4 oz caster sugar
100 g/4 oz plain flour, sifted
175 g/6 oz whole, unblanched almonds

Heat the oven to moderate, 180°C/350°F, Gas Mark 4. In a bowl, beat the egg whites until they hold stiff peaks. Gradually beat in the sugar until the mixture has a meringue-like consistency. Fold in the flour and almonds. Mix lightly.

Place the mixture into a buttered and floured 23 cm/9 inch loaf tin. Bake in the centre of the oven for 30-40 minutes, or until firm to the touch. Turn out on a wire rack and leave to cool. Wrap in foil and leave for 2 days.

Heat the oven to very cool, 110°C/220°F, Gas Mark ¼. Cut the loaf in wafer-thin slices. Place the slices on oven trays and bake in the oven for 45 minutes, or until crisp and lightly coloured. Cool on a wire rack.

VANILLA BISCUITS

MAKES ABOUT 70

2 eggs
225 g/8 oz sugar
100 g/4 oz soft butter
½ teaspoon bicarbonate of soda
1 teaspoon vanilla essence
225 g/8 oz plain flour
caster sugar, for dusting

Heat the oven to moderate, 180°C/350°F, Gas Mark 4. Beat the eggs and sugar until pale and thick. Beat in the butter, a little at a time. Add the bicarbonate of soda and vanilla. Beat in the flour. The mixture should be stiff: add a little more flour if necessary.

Roll out the dough on a lightly floured board and cut in small, thin rounds. Sprinkle with caster sugar and place on a greased baking sheet. Bake on the centre shelf for 12-15 minutes, or until the biscuits are slightly browned. Remove from oven and cool. Store in an airtight container.

Fill the pastry cases for Apple Cream Tarts just before serving.

APPLE CREAM TARTS

MAKES 24

PASTRY:
200 g/7 oz self-raising flour
175 g/6 oz cold butter, cut in cubes
1½ tablespoons icing sugar

APPLE CREAM FILLING:
4 Granny Smith apples, peeled, seeded
  and sliced
100 g/4 oz sugar
300 ml/½ pint double cream
1 teaspoon vanilla essence
1 tablespoon caster sugar or to taste

TO MAKE THE PASTRY CASES: put the flour, butter and icing sugar in a food processor and process until mixture forms a ball. Remove from the processor bowl, wrap in clingfilm and refrigerate for 2 hours.

Heat the oven to moderately hot, 190°C/375°F, Gas Mark 5. Lightly grease 24 muffin tins with vegetable oil. Roll out the pastry in small amounts at a time, and cut with a 7.5 cm/3 inch round cutter to make deep tarts. Line the tins with pastry and cook on the second bottom shelf of the oven for 12-15 minutes or until the cases are crisp and golden brown. Carefully turn out on to a rack to cool. The cases will keep fresh for 3-4 days in an airtight container.

TO MAKE THE APPLE CREAM: cook the apples over a moderate heat with a little water until mushy. Add the sugar, and cook until all the liquid is absorbed. Allow to cool. Beat the cream with the vanilla essence and sugar and mix with the cooled apple. Spoon the cream into the tarts just before serving.

87

OUTDOOR DRINKS

*Iced teas and fruit cups, coolers
and heady cocktails to sip all summer through*

Outdoor entertaining demands that you serve drinks that have a special flair. Dinners indoors deserve the best wines and require a more conservative approach but with barbecues and picnics, you can afford to experiment, be a little different, selecting drinks that add to the carefree enjoyment of entertaining al fresco.

The choice of these drinks will be limited only by your imagination and the facilities available. Obviously, a patio barbecue with a well-stocked bar within easy reach gives more scope than if you are packing for a picnic far from the usual mod cons.

You may prefer to make up just one drink and usually this can be prepared in advance to give you more time to enjoy your guests. This may be served throughout or just as a welcoming start. Sangria or Bloody Marys are good examples.

Wines may be served simply or mixed into coolers or a punch. Champagne is always the right choice, whether made up into a special drink such as Vogue Fizz or Kir Royale, or simply chilled.

Cater for beer lovers with a selection of local and imported brews, including low-alcohol varieties for those who prefer them. Cans are easiest for storage and best for easy transport to picnics.

Remember to supply a selection of mineral water, fruit juices (and perhaps that old favourite barley water) and other non-alcoholic drinks for those who enjoy them and those who recognise they are often the best thirst-quenchers of all. A choice of tea and coffee should also be available; use your imagination to make some interesting variations, whether hot or cold.

Drinks may be decorated with fresh fruit, herbs and flowers. Avoid the temptation to over-ornament; punch containers shouldn't resemble fruit barrows or flower gardens. Here an attractive centrepiece is all that is needed to highlight a fruit cocktail in a simple glass jug.

EVEREST ICED TEA

SERVES 6

7 teaspoons Darjeeling tea
crushed ice
sugar
lemon slices

Make the tea in the usual way: warm a 1.2 litre/2 pint teapot, place the tea leaves in it, and pour on boiling water as soon as it comes to the boil. Stir once or twice, put the lid on the pot and leave to infuse for 5 minutes. For each person fill a tall glass with crushed ice. Strain the tea on to the ice. Add sugar and lemon to taste. Cool for 1-2 minutes. Stir with a long-handled spoon and serve.

ICED TEA COCKTAILS

SERVES 12

Everest Iced Tea (see above)
fresh fruit juice of your choice (such as
*   citrus fruit or pineapple)*
ginger ale or soda

TO SERVE:
chopped fresh fruit
sprigs of mint

Prepare Everest Iced Tea but only fill the glasses half way. Add fruit juice and top up with ginger ale or soda. Stir once and serve, decorated with a little chopped fruit and a sprig of mint.

SHALIMAR TEA FRUIT CUP

MAKES 2.5-3 LITRES/4½-5½ PINTS

150 g/5 oz sugar
1 litre/1¾ pints water
4 tablespoons strong, fresh Assam tea,
*   cooled slightly*
120 ml/4 fl oz fruit syrup of your choice
4 tablespoons lemon juice
120 ml/4 fl oz fresh orange juice
120 ml/4 fl oz pineapple juice
1 small bottle lemonade
12 cherries, fresh or canned, stones
*   removed*
2 sliced bananas

Place the sugar in a small saucepan with 4 tablespoons water. Bring the water to the boil, stirring all the time to dissolve the sugar. Boil for 5 minutes. Away from the heat stir in the tea, syrup, fruit juices and the rest of the water. Transfer the fruit cup to a jug and chill in the refrigerator for about 30 minutes. To serve, add the lemonade, cherries and the sliced bananas.

BARLEY WATER

MAKES 2.5 LITRES/4½ PINTS
50 g/2 oz pearl barley
25 g/1 oz sugar
rind and juice of 1 lemon
2 litres/3½ pints boiling water

Wash the barley and blanch by placing in a large saucepan of cold water, bringing to the boil and boiling for 1 minute. Strain, discarding the liquid. Add the sugar and lemon rind and juice to the barley. Pour over the freshly boiling water, cover and leave to cool. Strain the barley water and chill before serving.

FRESH FRUIT COCKTAIL

MAKES 4

crushed ice
250 g/9 oz fresh fruit in season, puréed
juice of 1 orange
juice of 1 lemon
soda water

Place crushed ice in the bottom of tall glasses. Divide the fruit purée between the glasses, then the fruit juices, and fill up with soda water.

MINT DRINK

TO MAKE 1.25 LITRES/2¼ PINTS

1.5 kg/3 Lb sugar
750 ml/1¼ pints water
juice and rind of 2 lemons
250 ml/8 fl oz white vinegar
2 large handfuls of mint leaves, washed
*   and drained*

TO SERVE:
ice cubes
soda
cucumber slices or borage leaves and
*   flowers*

Dissolve the sugar in the water in a saucepan and bring slowly to the boil, stirring constantly. Add the lemon juice and rind and vinegar. Reduce the heat and simmer for 20 minutes. Add the mint leaves, and return to the boil for 1 minute. Remove from the heat and leave to cool. Strain.
TO SERVE: fill a jug or glass one-third full with the mint syrup, about one-third of ice cubes and finally, top up with soda.
    Decorate with cucumber slices or fresh borage leaves and flowers.

A long cool drink for any occasion – Strawberry Grapefruit Punch.

STRAWBERRY GRAPEFRUIT PUNCH

SERVES 10-12

1 tablespoon honey
2 tablespoons peppermint tea or mint-
* flavoured Indian tea*
500 g/1¼ lb strawberries, hulled
600 ml/1 pint fresh grapefruit juice
1.5 litres/2½ pints cold water

Dissolve the honey in the freshly made tea. Place in a blender with the strawberries and fruit juice. Blend to make a purée. Add the cold water and blend again. Transfer to a jug and chill for 30 minutes before serving.

BALM AMBROSIA

MAKES 2 LITRES/3½ PINTS

100 g/4 oz sugar
750 ml/1¼ pints water
sprigs of balm
juice of 3 oranges
juice of 1 lemon
1 litre/1¾ pints canned pineapple juice

Place the sugar, water and some of the balm in a saucepan. Simmer for 5 minutes to dissolve the sugar and extract the balm fragrance. Strain into a jug, discarding the balm. Add a few long, fresh sprays of balm and fruit juices. Chill.

SANGRIA

SERVES 6-8

500 ml/18 fl oz orange juice
250 ml/8 fl oz lemon juice
sugar to taste
1 orange, sliced thinly
1 lemon, sliced thinly
1 bottle red wine
ice cubes (optional)

In a glass bowl or jug, combine the juices and sweeten to taste. Add the sliced fruit and stand the jug in the refrigerator for 1 hour. Before serving, add the red wine and mix well. To serve, ladle the wine into chilled tumblers, including a little fruit and ice cubes if desired. Do not add ice to the jug as it will dilute the Sangria.

WILD APPLE COOLER

MAKES 1

1 measure Calvados
1 measure Galliano
2 measures guava juice
3 measures apple juice
ice cubes

Blend the liqueurs and fruit juices together in a blender or cocktail shaker. Fill a long glass with ice cubes and pour the liquid over the top.

WHITE WINE WITH ESSENCE OF ORANGE

MAKES ABOUT 1.25 LITRES/2¼ PINTS

8 large oranges, to yield about 100 g/4 oz dried peel (see recipe)
2 cloves
small piece of cinnamon bark
1.25 litres/2¼ pints dry white wine
75-100 g/3-4 oz sugar, to taste
3-4 tablespoons good cognac

To dry the orange peel, peel the skin from the oranges, avoiding the bitter white pith. Spread it out to dry. In an open area, it will dry in a few days to a week, depending on humidity.

Put the dried orange peel, cloves and cinnamon in a jug. Pour in the wine. Cover and set in a cool place away from the light to macerate for 8-10 days until the wine is imbued with the taste of orange.

Strain the wine. Pour 250 ml/8 fl oz into an enamelled saucepan, add sugar to taste, and stir over a gentle heat without allowing the mixture to boil, until the sugar has melted. Pour back into the wine in a jug, add the cognac and stir.

The wine can be served at once or kept in corked wine bottles. Serve very cold with a sliver of fresh orange peel to decorate each glass.

KIR ROYALE

SERVES 4

4 teaspoons cassis
1 bottle champagne

Swirl 1 teaspoon of cassis around each of 4 glasses and top up with chilled champagne. Serve immediately.

LOVING CUP

MAKES ABOUT 16 DRINKS

2 lemons
several sugar cubes
a few leaves of balm
a sprig of borage
900 ml/1½ pints water
½ bottle Madeira
150 ml/¼ pint brandy
1 bottle champagne

Rub the peel of 1 lemon with sugar cubes, turning them so that they absorb the oil of the zest. Peel both lemons, discarding the peel. Cut the lemons into thin slices and place with the balm leaves and borage in a jug with the lemon sugar. Add water, madeira and brandy. Cover and chill for 1 hour. Just before serving, add the bottle of chilled champagne.

CHAMPAGNE PUNCH

MAKES AT LEAST 40 DRINKS

3 ripe pineapples, peeled and cored
400 g/1 lb caster sugar
500 ml/18 fl oz lemon juice
350 ml/12 fl oz white Curaçao
225 g/8 oz chopped cherries
1 litre/1¾ pints white rum
4 bottles champagne, chilled

Chop the pineapples finely in a food processor or by hand. Add the sugar, lemon juice, curaçao, cherries and rum. Transfer to a jug, cover and let it stand in the refrigerator for 2-3 hours to chill thoroughly. To serve, pour the punch over a block of ice in a large bowl. Add the chilled champagne.

An imaginative and refreshing welcome: glasses of Fresh Fruit in Champagne.

FRESH FRUIT IN CHAMPAGNE

SERVES 4

450 g/1 lb mixed fresh fruit in season
1 bottle champagne, chilled

Choose fruits with an eye to colour, and to vary the texture. Prepare each according to type and cut into pieces of roughly equal size if necessary. Fill 4 champagne flutes with the prepared fruit. Pour over the chilled champagne and serve the drinks with long straws.

VOGUE FIZZ

MAKES 4

8 passionfruit
100 g/4 oz caster sugar
4 sugar lumps
bitters
juice of 1 lime
crushed ice
1 bottle champagne, chilled

Scoop out the passionfruit into a sieve set over a bowl. Strain out all the seeds and discard. Add the caster sugar to the passionfruit purée and stir well to dissolve.

Into each of 4 chilled champagne glasses place a lump of sugar soaked with a drop of bitters. Divide the fruit syrup and lime juice between the glasses. Add crushed ice, top each glass up with champagne and serve.

BLOODY MARY

MAKES 1

*1 measure vodka
2-3 ice cubes
pinch celery salt
pinch ground white pepper
¾ teaspoon Worcestershire sauce
few drops Tabasco sauce, to taste
1 slice of lime or lemon
tomato juice*

Pour the vodka into a tall glass and add the ice cubes. Add the celery salt, pepper, Worcestershire sauce and Tabasco sauce. Twist the slice of lime or lemon over the glass to extract the juice, then drop the slice into the glass. Mix thoroughly with a swizzle stick, pressing the lime slice to extract more juice. Top up with tomato juice and stir again to combine.

VARIATIONS FOR BLOODY MARY

Top up the glass with 2 parts tomato juice and 1 part V-8 vegetable juice. This gives the drink added flavour.

For a party, prepare the tomato juice mixture without vodka, ice or lime slices (squeeze lime juice into the mixture instead). Have a decanter of vodka, ice, lime slices and spoons at hand for mixing individual drinks.

PINA COLADA

MAKES 2

*1½ tablespoons creamed coconut
3 tablespoons white rum
5 tablespoons unsweetened fresh
  pineapple juice
250 ml/8 fl oz crushed ice*

Place all the ingredients in a blender and combine, or shake them very well in a cocktail shaker, until the liquid is frothy. Pour into wine glasses.

FROZEN MARGUERITA

MAKES 1

*salt
3 tablespoons tequila
4 teaspoons fresh lemon juice
dash of Cointreau*

TO SERVE:
crushed ice and lemon twist

Rim a stemmed glass or a champagne glass with salt. Mix the ingredients in the glass with a swizzle stick. Add crushed ice and serve with a twist of lemon.

MINT JULEP

MAKES 1

*1 teaspoon sugar
4 mint sprigs
crushed ice
1 measure bourbon whisky*

Dissolve the sugar in a teaspoon of water in a tumbler. Take 3 mint sprigs and crush them lightly between your fingers. Put them in the tumbler and fill it three-quarters full with crushed ice. Add the bourbon and tuck the remaining mint sprig into the ice. Chill until the tumbler is frosted.

STRAWBERRY RUM DAIQUIRI

MAKES 1

*50-75 g/2-3 oz strawberries, sliced
3 tablespoons light rum
1 teaspoon lemon juice
1 teaspoon sugar
250 ml/8 fl oz cracked ice*

TO DECORATE:
*1 strawberry
twist of lemon*

Blend all the ingredients for about 20 seconds. Pour into a long glass and garnish with a strawberry and a twist of lemon.

TIE BREAKER

MAKES 1

*3 fresh strawberries
4 teaspoons Fraise de Bordeaux
  (strawberry liqueur)
3 teaspoons Cointreau
dash of lemon juice*

TO SERVE:
*crushed ice
champagne, to top
1 small strawberry*

Blend all the ingredients with 1 small scoop of crushed ice. Pour into a bowl-shaped glass and top with chilled champagne. Add straws and decorate with a strawberry.

INDEX